Train Up a Child

Successful Parenting for the Next Generation

DANIEL L. SWITZER, Ed. D.

With a Foreword by

DAVID J. RUDOLPH, Ph. D.

Lederer Books
A division of
Messianic Jewish Publishers
Clarksville, Maryland

Scripture quotations are taken from:

Complete Jewish Bible © 1998 by David H. Stern,
Published by Jewish New Testament Publications, Inc.,

The Holy Bible, New International Version® NIV®.
© 1973, 1978, 1984 by International Bible Society

The *New Covenant Prophecy Edition*
© 1973, 1978, 1984, 1991 by International Bible Society.

Used by permission. All rights reserved worldwide.

Cover Design by
Josh Huhn, Design Point, Inc.

12 11 10 09 08 07   6 5 4 3 2 1

ISBN 13: 978-1-880226-37-5
ISBN 10: 1-880226-37-5

Library of Congress Control Number: 2007925884
Printed in the United States of America

Lederer Books
A division of
Messianic Jewish Publishers
6120 Day Long Lane
Clarksville, Maryland 21029

Distributed by
Messianic Jewish Resources International
Order Line: (800) 410-7367
E-mail: lederer@messianicjewish.net
Website: www.messianicjewish.net

"Children's children are a crown to the aged,
and parents are the pride of their children."
(Prov. 17:6)

This book is dedicated to my parents,
Thurlow and Lynda Switzer,
who faithfully and lovingly raised their four sons
on principles from the Word of God.
I thank them and honor them for their love,
their example, their godly conviction,
and their transparent relationship with the Lord.

Contents

Acknowledgments

I WOULD LIKE TO THANK a number of people who contributed to making this book a reality. My friend David Rudolph encouraged me throughout the process of submission, writing, and revisions. He also graciously provided me with technical expertise and with final editing.

I am very grateful to the men's discipleship team at Northgate Community Church in Gaithersburg, Maryland, for their encouragement. Their prayers provided me with personal motivation during the process.

I very much appreciate Barry Rubin, president of Messianic Jewish Publishers, for his guidance and support. He challenged me to pursue excellence with the manuscript. His executive assistant, Rebecca Hoffman, helped greatly in facilitating the process of revisions. Joshua Rosenthal patiently worked with me in honing my writing.

My wife, Silvia Switzer, was instrumental in helping me organize the content in the most effective way and provided me with many anecdotes for the book. Silvia is a treasure, a helpmate in the truest sense of the word, and a grace-filled mother to our four children.

Finally, I give the Lord all glory for the privilege to share what he has taught me. I am exceedingly grateful for his capturing my life by his grace and consider it an honor to be called his friend.

Foreword

I REMEMBER THE MONTHS BEFORE Dan Switzer's first child was born. Dan was like a rocket waiting to blast off into the world of parenthood. He couldn't wait. It was as though his destiny in life was about to be fulfilled. When Anna was finally born, Dan's love poured into Anna like water from a pitcher. Dan was now a father and the happiest man alive.

God created the parent-child relationship to reflect a relational love that exists within God himself. For this reason, we must regularly return to God and his Word to understand how to be loving parents. Dan Switzer knows the importance of this truth. He has sought the Lord again and again for wisdom to train up children in the Lord; and now he has made his findings available to us in *Train Up a Child*, a veritable treasure chest of the wisdom and experience Dr. Switzer has collected over the years.

Train Up a Child is unique in several regards. First, it draws deeply from biblical sources. On almost every page, scriptures are quoted and elucidated so that the reader can hear God's Word and be encouraged by it. Parents would do well to underline these biblical passages and memorize them as a way of internalizing this divine wisdom and counsel.

Second, because Dr. Switzer was the principal of a Messianic Jewish day school for eleven years, the wisdom of the Jewish sages informs his approach to child rearing. This adds to the richness of *Train Up a Child* and sets it apart from most other parenting guides. At the same time, because Dr. Switzer's family and church background are not Messianic Jewish but Christian, he is able to speak more broadly to the experience of Jews and Gentiles in the Body of Messiah.

A third distinction of *Train Up a Child* is the personal experience that Dr. Switzer brings to bear on the subject of parenting. In addition to having served as a school principal, Dr. Switzer is a pastor, a summer camp director, a soccer and basketball coach, and the father of four children. Dr. Switzer does not present us with mere theory in his book, but also time-tested wisdom that has worked for countless parents.

Over the past ten years, I have had the privilege of serving with Dan in various capacities and I commend him to the reader as one of the most Yeshua-like people I have ever known. He is pure-hearted and humble, a *mentsch* [good person] in the fullest sense of the word. One of his favorite scriptures is Galatians 2:20, "I have been crucified with Messiah and I no longer live, but Messiah lives in me. The life I live in the body, I live by faith in the Son of God, who loved me and gave himself for me."

My sense is that Dan's passion for parenting is ultimately rooted in his identification with the crucified and risen Messiah who revealed the Father's love to his disciples (John 14:9). Dan and his wife Silvia view their children as beloved disciples whom the Lord has entrusted into their parental care. Is this not how we should view our own children, as beloved disciples? I would encourage the reader to step back and allow Dr. Switzer, through his book, to disciple you in how to disciple your own children. You will be learning from a master.

DAVID J. RUDOLPH, Ph.D. (Cambridge)

Introduction

WHEN EACH OF MY FOUR CHILDREN WAS BORN, I was ener-gized for life. The inspiration that came with the birth of my children motivated me to improve every aspect of my life. Even my commitment to the Lord was renewed.

The night my son Caleb was born, I went home and fell on my knees to pray. My prayer expressed my desire to be an example of God's love to my son in order to train him in the way he should go. I committed myself to being a faithful steward of the time God gives me with him on this earth. I was filled with purpose.

Because I am a principal working in a Messianic Jewish school, parents often share their experiences with me. I have learned from these conversations that having a child often changes a person's perspective. The sudden responsibility for this precious life helps mothers and fathers realize that they have to change their lives. Having a child often motivates parents to get right with God, to get their lives in order, and to seek counsel regarding child raising.

My goal in writing this book is to equip parents with God-given tools to train up their children. My desire is that parents will embrace this task with the confidence that only God can provide. With parenting children, as with any great endeavor, it is essen-tial to understand our purpose. And for purpose we turn to the Scriptures. God has given the Scriptures to us to be our guidebook for living. They express timeless truths that, if applied, will result in blessing. They provide parents with purpose and motivation for raising children.

Why do we go through the daily effort to train and instruct our children? The *Sh'ma* (Deuteronomy 6:4–9) helps to answer this question:

> *Sh'ma, Yisra'el!* ADONAI *Eloheinu,* ADONAI *echad* [Hear, Isra'el! ADONAI our God, ADONAI is one]; and you are to love ADONAI your God with all your heart, all your being and all your resources. These words, which I am ordering you today, are to be on your heart; and you are to teach them carefully to your children. You are to talk about them when you sit at home, when you are traveling on the road, when you lie down and when you get up. Tie them on your hand as a sign, put them at the front of a headband around your forehead, and write them on the door-frames of your house and on your gates.

Our calling is to teach our children to love God with every aspect of their being. When asked about the most important commandment, Yeshua repeated the *Sh'ma* and said that we are to love God with all of our heart, soul, mind, and strength. Likewise, parenting our children should focus on these areas. A concern for the heart, for instance, would be to develop our child's sensitivity to the Lord in worship. Regarding the soul, we can help our children to serve God with passion. With respect to the mind, we can counsel our young people to understand that the spiritual battle is won or lost in the thought realm; they must learn to take captive every thought to make it obedient to Messiah. Our children can learn to love God with all of their heart, soul, understanding, and strength as they play on their soccer team, study at school, or spend time with friends. A major part of helping children develop a love for the Lord is teaching them to give their all to him. Colossians 3:23 says, "Whatever you do, work at it *with all your heart, as working for the Lord,* not for men" (italics added). Loving God is giving our all to him!

Our son, Caleb, who seems to virtually drink up our love for him, takes everything we say to heart. When I coached Caleb's basketball team, I encouraged him to play with everything he had for Messiah. I saw my son applying what I taught him, to love God with his whole heart, soul, mind, and strength, in everything he does.

We need to learn to give our all for Yeshua. Loving God with everything we have, and helping our children gain that kind of heart, fills me with purpose as a parent. People who love God live excellently; they give one hundred percent to him!

In addition, as the *Sh'ma* indicates, we should interact with God's Word all day long: at the beginning of the day, during the day, and at the end of the day. We should look for opportunities to write God's principles on our children's hearts. One of my cherished memories is of my mother praying with me at my bedside before I would go to sleep. She would take the time to talk with me, to help resolve the cares of the day, and to build me up in the Lord.

Have you ever considered that Yeshua's directive in Matthew 28:19–20 entails a significant mission for parents? Yeshua told his *talmidim* [disciples] to make other disciples and to teach them to obey his commands. Surely our children should be our first disciples. They need to be continually challenged to draw near to Yeshua. This relationship with him is cultivated through prayer, Scripture reading, worship, and exercising faith as they grow in their consciousness of the Lord's presence in their lives. We need to remember that God is with us as we disciple our children.

The principles outlined in this book will equip you as a parent. I use many anecdotes from my work at school, as well as from my family life, to illustrate how these principles are applied. Many of these stories are from journals I have kept for each of my children.

My assumption throughout the book is that you are a parent. I share with you as one parent speaking to another about this tremendous adventure of training our children in the Lord.

Part One

Biblical Principles
of Parenting

GOD'S WORD NEEDS TO PERMEATE our lives and make a difference in how we relate to our children. Through reading and internalizing his Word, we understand how God relates to us as a loving Father. This in turn helps us to have a healthy and balanced perspective toward our own children. Romans 8:15–16 reminds us of our parent-child relationship with God:

> For you did not receive a spirit of slavery to bring you back again into fear; on the contrary, you received the Spirit, who makes us sons and by whose power we cry out, "Abba!" (that is, "Dear Father!"). The Spirit himself bears witness with our own spirits that we are children of God.

With this perspective in mind, we will address the following biblical principles: our responsibility, having an accurate view of God, living according to the Scriptures, having a vision for each child, respecting authority, using our authority, and declaring the victory of Messiah.

Chapter One

Our Responsibility

T HE SCRIPTURES TELL US that parents have a sacred responsibility to teach their children. Deuteronomy 11:19 calls parents to "teach [God's words] carefully to your children, talking about them when you sit at home, when you are traveling along the road, when you lie down and when you get up." This is to be a continual activity each day. Proverbs 22:6 teaches, "Train a child in the way he should go, and when he is old he will not turn from it." Ephesians 6:4 directs fathers to "bring [their children] up in the training and instruction of the Lord." God's expectation is that we would embrace the responsibility to train and instruct our children. As Rabbi Abraham Twersky and Ursula Schwartz remind us, we are accountable for these precious lives entrusted to our care:

> With G-d as an intimate partner in parenting, we can no longer talk of "having" a child in the simple possessive fashion implied by ordinary language. Rather, having a child means to be entrusted with a responsibility. A child is a gift of G-d chosen for us specifically and entrusted to us for safekeeping to be raised and treasured. (Twerski and Schwartz, 24)

I recall my excitement when my wife, Silvia, told me that she was pregnant with our first child. Silvia had had trouble conceiving. For years, we prayed for a baby. Well, with the news of her pregnancy and with the subsequent birth of our daughter, Anna, we were overjoyed with this gift from God. For me, the birth of our daughter was a spiritual experience; I felt the Lord inspiring me as a new father. If you've had children, I'm sure you can relate to this.

Anna was a trust bestowed by the Lord, and not to be taken lightly. My wife and I embraced the seriousness of our task to train her in the Lord. I felt that I could tell by the look in my daughter's face that she was filled with purpose, resolve, and courage for her life ahead. On the way home from the hospital, I cried tears of joy for her, and I committed her into the Lord's hands.

Our Motivation

Psalm 78:1–7 provides us with motivation to instruct the generations to come about the Lord:

> Listen, my people, to my teaching; turn your ears to the words from my mouth. I will speak to you in parables and explain mysteries from days of old. The things which we have heard and known, and which our fathers told us we will not hide from their descendants; we will tell the generation to come the praises of ADONAI and his strength, the wonders that he has performed. He raised up a testimony in Ya'akov [Jacob] and established a Torah in Isra'el. He commanded our ancestors to make this known to their children, so that the next generation would know it, the children not yet born, who would themselves arise and tell their own children, who could then put their confidence in God, not forgetting God's deeds, but obeying his mitzvot.

I am grateful to my great-grandfather who gave his life to the Lord and to my grandfather who was a man of God. He and my grandmother raised my father, who with my mother, faithfully raised my brothers and me in the Lord. And now Silvia and I are seeking to train our children according to God's Word.

God's transgenerational purpose is compelling. The next generation needs to learn his decrees. Our children need to know their Creator and understand how he created them to live, for this will prepare them to raise up the next generation for the Lord.

God's Command to Children

Just as God instructs parents to teach their children, he instructs children to obey and honor their parents–and for good reason! Colossians 3:20 says, "Children, obey your parents in everything; for this pleases the Lord." God expects our children to obey us in all things as long as we are faithfully following Yeshua the Messiah: "Children, obey your parents in the Lord, for this is right" (Eph. 6:1).

Furthermore, there is strong incentive for our children to honor us, as the fifth of the Ten Commandments clearly states, "Honor your father and mother, as ADONAI your God ordered you to do, so that you will live long and have things go well with you in the land ADONAI your God is giving you" (Deut. 5:16). This commandment's promise is restated in Ephesians 6:3, "that it may go well with you and that you may enjoy long life on the earth."

Honoring parents is as serious as the duty to honor God himself:

> The Rabbis learned: It says, "Honor your father and your mother" (Shemot [Exodus] 20:11), and it also says, "Honor HaShem [The Lord] with your money" (Mishlei [Proverbs] 3:9). The Torah made the honor one must show to one's mother and father equivalent to the honor given to HaShem.
>
> It says, "A man should be in awe of his father and his mother" (Vayikra [Leviticus] 19:3), and it also says, "You should be in awe of HaShem, your God" (Devarim [Deuteronomy] 12:20). The Torah made the awe one must have for one's mother and father equivalent to the awe of HaShem. (Ta'aseh, 136)

The command to honor parents should be treated as just that—a command from God. It is not an option; it is a serious matter before the Lord for children to honor their parents. Those children who fulfill this command will experience blessing throughout their lifetime.

A Serious Responsibility

The Scriptures describe in graphic language the severe consequences of not teaching and training children. If we do not teach children according to God's Word, it is as if we are cursing them. The Book of Proverbs is filled with references to "my son" and provides much motivation for parents to take their role seriously. For example, Proverbs 29:15b says, "A child left to himself brings shame on his mother."

1 Samuel 3:13 expresses the consequences of Eli's failure to restrain his children: "For I told him that I would judge his family forever because of the sin he knew about; his sons made themselves contemptible, and he failed to restrain them." Eventually, God's judgment upon Eli's family impacted the entire nation: "The P'lishtim fought, Isra'el was defeated, and every man fled to his tent. It was a terrible slaughter—30,000 of Isra'el's foot soldiers fell. Moreover, the ark of God was captured; and the two sons of 'Eli, Hofni and Pinchas, died" (I Sam. 4:10–11).

We are responsible for what influences our children; blame cannot be passed on to anyone or anything else. Judges 2:10–11 describes the failure of a generation of parents and the consequences of that failure:

> When that entire generation had been gathered to their ancestors, another generation arose that knew neither ADO- NAI nor the work he had done for Isra'el. Then the people of Isra'el did what was evil from ADONAI's perspective and served the *ba'alim* [foreign gods].

On the other hand, if we take our responsibility seriously, we will experience God's blessing. Many proverbs speak of the positive results of biblical parenting. Proverbs 29:17 encourages us, "Discipline your son, and he will give you rest; yes, he will be your delight." If we are faithful to teach and discipline our children, we will eventually see the blessing.

Have Faith in God

Habakkuk 2:4 says, "The righteous will attain life through trusting faithfulness." As believers in Yeshua the Messiah we are called to live by faith. In fact, our father Abraham was declared righteous because he believed God. We need to walk in the faith God gives us while raising our children.

As we apply God's Word in training our children, and pray for God's work to be done in their lives, the Lord will show himself faithful. Esther 2:7 says of Mordecai that "he had raised Hadassah, that is, Ester, his uncle's daughter." Here, the Hebrew word for "raised" is a cognate of the Hebrew word for "faith." As Rabbi Shmuel Brog notes, "All of *chinuch* (training) is rooted in a sense of faith on the part of the parent and educator; faith in the innate potential of the child and a belief that, eventually, all that is good and beautiful in him will flourish" (Cohen, xxx). Our work is indeed an adventure of faith!

Chapter Two

An Accurate View of God

THERE ARE MANY DIFFERENT VIEWS of God in our society today. When a tragedy occurs, some people question the existence of God, for "how could a loving God allow such a terrible thing to happen?" Others have grown up without experiencing the consequences of their wrongdoing; thus, they do not believe that God would actually punish them for their sin, and, besides, "a loving God would not do such a thing." These perspectives fail to recognize that God created mankind with the freedom to choose or reject him. They also fail to recognize the consequences of sin.

It is important to have an accurate view of God. Understanding God's heart for his children can help us to understand the perspective that we are supposed to have toward our children. For example, Jeremiah 31:20 tells us that God delights in his children:

> Isn't Efrayim my very dear son, a child who delights me so?
> I speak about him all the time; I can't help but recall him
> to mind. In sum, I deeply yearn for him; I will surely show
> him favor, says ADONAI.

Yeshua delighted in children. He said, "Let the little children come to me, and do not hinder them, for the kingdom of heaven belongs to such as these" (Matt. 19:14).

When my son Nehemiah was a toddler, we wrestled together with lots of tickling and laughing. It was an opportunity for me to communicate my delight to him. One particular evening, Nehemiah saw my eyes like never before. I took off my glasses, and my son peered deeply into my eyes. He seemed to discover something that he had never seen before. He and I stopped our wrestling and took time to share our love with each other. About a year later, we had a similar experience, but this time Nehemiah saw himself in my eyes. Silvia and I had a good laugh when he told his cousin to look into my eyes to see himself. Nehemiah now thinks that his image is permanently etched in my eyes. As parents, we need to communicate delight to our children.

Our Lord welcomes us as his children, even when we have been disobedient. Yeshua's parable of the wayward son and his father's response to his son's return is powerful: "But while he [the wayward son] was still a long way off, his father saw him and was moved with pity. He ran and threw his arms around him and kissed him warmly" (Luke 15:20).

God's knowledge of us, and love for us, knows no bounds. Psalm 139 expresses the extent of God's care for us:

> O Lord, you have searched me and you know me. You know when I sit and when I rise; you perceive my thoughts from afar. You discern my going out and my lying down; you are familiar with all my ways. Before a word is on my tongue you know it completely, O Lord. You hem me in–behind and before; you have laid your hand upon me. Such knowledge is too wonderful for me, too lofty for me to attain . . . . For you created my inmost being; you knit me together in my mother's womb. I praise you because I am fearfully and wonderfully made; your works are wonderful, I know that full well. My frame was not hidden from you when I was made in the secret place. When I was woven together in the depths of the earth, your eyes saw my unformed body. All the days ordained for me were written in your book before one of them came to be. (Ps. 139:1–6, 13–16)

Clearly, God knows, loves, and considers each one of his children to be special. We need to emulate this example.

As our children work through life experiences, it is important that we communicate the heart of God to them, even when they miss the mark. When one of our sons was six years old, he came to us and was very troubled about something he had done. He confessed a very serious offense. While we were saddened about the sin, we were careful to communicate our unconditional love for him. Later we helped him to take responsibility for what he had done, but he still knew that we loved him "no matter what." Our son knew that his relationship of love with his parents was intact.

We can learn much about relating to our children by studying how our Father relates to us. The question is not whether we are perfectly emulating God before our children; it is whether we are building a trusting relationship with them, born out of love, instead of fear. Do we regularly communicate delight over our children? Do they know that we love them no matter what? Knowing God's heart toward us enables us to communicate this kind of love toward our children.

Helping Our Children Receive God's Love

We can best help our children grow in the love of God when we have an accurate view of God. With this knowledge, we should stress God's love for our children and our love for them from their infancy. My wife and I have done this in a very passionate manner. We excitedly say things like, "I love you *soooo* much!" When my daughter was three years old, she showed us that she was getting the message by coining a new expression for our family: "I love you so much and more!" I have often sought to communicate our Father's great love to my children at the same time that I am communicating my personal love for them.

As our children are able to understand God's love for them, they will be able to love others. We can help them in this endeavor. Romans 13:9–10 says, "For the commandments . . . are summed up in this one rule: 'Love your neighbor as yourself.' Love does not do harm to a neighbor; therefore love is the fullness of Torah."

Our children need to focus on loving others, instead of selfishly focusing on their own desires.

Any parent with several children knows the challenge of sibling rivalry. Sibling rivalry can be frustrating, but it does provide an opportunity to train our children to love their neighbor. They need to start with loving their brothers and sisters! As a parent of four, it seems that I am constantly telling my children to live in harmony and to walk in peace with one another. As Psalm 34:15 challenges us, "Seek peace, go after it!"

The name of my third child, Nehemiah, means "the Lord's comfort." Well, he likes to "comfort" his older brother by tackling him and wrestling with him! Fortunately, Caleb is very indulgent toward his younger brother; he is becoming a boy who loves his neighbor. (At the same time, Silvia and I are working very hard to help Nehemiah understand when it is appropriate and when it is not appropriate to tackle and wrestle others.)

A Healthy Fear of God

An accurate view of God leads to a healthy fear of God. This fear of God is not a cringing fear before some temperamental being who wants to destroy us. It is being in awe of the Creator of the universe, who dearly loves us.

When we revere God, we take to heart the seriousness of our responsibility. There is a blessing that God bestows on us and our children when we revere him: "But the mercy of ADONAI on those who fear him is from eternity past to eternity future, and his righteousness extends to his children's children, provided they keep his covenant and remember to follow his precepts" (Ps. 103:17–18).

Through revering God, we are able to impart to our children a healthy, biblical understanding of true guilt rather than false guilt. Romans 2:15 tells us, "The requirements of the law are written on their hearts, their consciences also bearing witness, and their thoughts now accusing, now even defending them." True guilt occurs when a law has been broken. It is an objective matter of right and wrong. God uses true guilt as a motivation for us to turn away from sin to him.

When I was a young driver, I was pulled over by the police while returning from a class I was taking with a friend. I had turned onto a main thoroughfare, rapidly increased my speed, and had broken the speed limit. For whatever reason, the police officer simply gave me a warning and let me go.

Later, while talking about the incident with my friend, I mentioned that I was going to tell my father about it. She was flabbergasted and asked why I would do such a thing. There was no reason to think my dad would find out. I responded that I couldn't keep such a thing from my father. My conscience wouldn't let me do it.

Well, I did tell my father about the incident and he did not react harshly. Instead, he gently counseled me about driving lawfully. Through that experience, my father built on the trust that existed between us. I became confident that I could share anything with him without fearing his reaction. I was able to deal with true guilt in a healthy manner and, in the process, keep a good conscience.

It is very important that we not react harshly when our children miss the mark. Otherwise, they will not trust us and will be tempted to hide the truth from us. We need to help them walk in true guilt and develop a healthy conscience through our patient and diligent instruction.

At the same time, some of our children will develop over-sensitive consciences: "This then is how we know that we belong to the truth, and how we set our hearts at rest in his presence whenever our hearts condemn us. For God is greater than our hearts, and he knows everything" (1 John 3:19–20). Hebrews 4:15 tells us that we have a high priest who is able "to sympathize with our weaknesses." Our children need to learn to enter the rest of God in which they are justified by faith (Heb. 4:1–11). God has perfect justice and perfect love. He has not given us rules so that he can whip us when we break one.

God designed life so that those who have a healthy fear of him will experience his blessing: "In the fear of ADONAI is powerful security; for his children there will be a place of refuge. The fear of ADONAI is a fountain of life enabling one to avoid deadly traps" (Prov. 14:26–27).

The Covenant of Marriage

As husbands and wives, it is foundational that we keep our covenant of love with each other. Genesis 2:24 says, "This is why a man is to leave his father and mother and stick with his wife, and they are to be one flesh." The marriage vow is a covenant between husband and wife, before God; it is a sacred promise. If broken, the consequences are severe, not only for us as spouses, but also for our children.

I am not just talking about divorce. The importance of the marriage covenant, expressed in unity and love in the home, is fundamental to our children's security. If there is no peace in the home, and our children are not secure, all of our good-intentioned efforts at bringing them up in the right way will be severely thwarted.

We see the breakdown of the family structure all around us. Malachi 2:15 expresses God's purpose for bringing husband and wife together within the marriage covenant: "Has not the Lord made them one? In flesh and spirit they are his. And why one? Because he was seeking godly offspring. So guard yourself in your spirit, and do not break faith with the wife of your youth." God has brought husband and wife together because he desires their children to have a heart for God. Malachi 2:16 emphasizes God's condemnation of divorce: "'I hate divorce,' says the Lord God of Israel."

Ephesians 5:25–33 speaks of a husband imitating Messiah by laying down his life for his wife and loving her as his own body. 1 Peter 3:7 exhorts husbands to be considerate toward their wives and to "treat them with respect . . . so that nothing will hinder your prayers." Colossians 3:19 commands husbands to "love your wives and don't treat them harshly." As we love each other according to the Scriptures, our children will be blessed in the process.

Walking in Covenant With Others

Finally, this covenantal way of relating needs to extend to others. Yeshua said, "I am giving you a new command: that you keep on loving each other. In the same way that I have loved you, you are also to keep on loving each other. Everyone will know that you are my *talmidim* by the fact that you have love for each other" (John 13:34–35). My parents, Thurlow and Lynda Switzer, in their *Parenting Is an Adventure Seminar*, emphasize the importance of Yeshua's teaching in Matthew 18 for understanding what it means to walk in covenant with others:

> Moreover, if your brother commits a sin against you, go and show him his fault – but privately, just between the two of you. If he doesn't listen, take one or two others with you so that every accusation can be supported by the testimony of two or three witnesses. If he refuses to hear them, tell the congregation; and if he refuses to listen even to the congregation, treat him as you would a pagan or a tax-collector . . . Then Kefa came up and said to him, "Rabbi, how often can my brother sin against me and I have to forgive him? As many as seven times?" "No, not seven times," answered Yeshua, "but seventy times seven!" (Matt. 18:15–17, 21–22)

As we seek to imitate Messiah in the spirit of unity and reconciliation, we will prosper in our relationships. This results in the blessing of abundant life for our children.

Chapter Three

Living According to the Scriptures

THE BEST THING we can do for our children is to live biblically. It is critical that we not make our faith a show for others to see. Children and teens can see right through parental hypocrisy. However, as we follow the Lord with sincerity of heart, our example will have a major impact.

The Power of Example

The influence that we have on our children cannot be overstated. John 5:19–20 says, "I tell you that the Son cannot do anything on his own, but only what he sees the Father doing; whatever the Father does, the Son does too. For the Father loves the Son and shows him everything he does." We can learn from the Father-Son relationship.

We all notice times when a boy does exactly what his father does; as the old saying goes, "Like father, like son." Whether it is working on a car, playing sports, or wearing a tie, we should show our children everything we do in love, just like our Father in heaven showed his Son Yeshua. As Yeshua emulated his Father, so too our children will naturally emulate us. The power of parental example is one of the strongest forces in our children's lives; all the more incentive for us to live according to God's Word!

This is important even at a very young age. When Anna was about sixteen months old, she saw an open Bible on the kitchen table and said "Bible." It was the first time her mother and I had heard her refer to God's Word in this way. Our children grow up "catching" who we are and what is important to us simply by their observation of our daily life and habits.

One specific way we can be godly examples to our children is by being grateful. I recall being convicted about my attitude toward giving my young children baths. Whether it was because I didn't like getting wet or because it was hard for me to be on my knees, I did not do this "chore" enthusiastically. I had a poor attitude. Well, the Lord convicted me about this attitude and the need to enjoy this stage of my children's lives. If we want them to develop an attitude of gratitude, then we need to show them an example of gratefulness. (As 1 Thessalonians 5:18 says, "Give thanks in all circumstances.")

Paul urged, "Try to imitate me, even as I myself try to imitate the Messiah" (1 Cor. 11:1). The Lord is our example, and I cannot overstate the need for us to be examples worth following. We parents are by definition leaders of our children. They ultimately will learn much more from our actions than from our words. Sinful habits and blind spots will be transferred to them if we are unwilling to honestly confront these areas in our lives.

One can almost hear the voice of God calling us to understand this principle, as expressed in Deuteronomy 5:29: "Oh, how I wish their hearts would stay like this always, that they would fear me and obey all my *mitzvot* so that it would go well with them and their children forever." The way we live in this generation will impact our children in the next generation. The importance of parental example is summed up in the Ten Commandments:

> You are not to bow down to them or serve them; for I, ADO-
> NAI your God, am a jealous God, punishing the children
> for the sins of the parents, also the third and fourth gen-
> eration of those who hate me, but displaying grace to the

thousandth generation of those who love me and obey my mitzvot. (Deut. 5:9–10)

Honesty is a very important issue. Children will catch dishonesty from us if we allow ourselves to tell "white lies." Allowing people who have not paid to share from a salad bar, or lying about our child's age so we can receive a cheaper fee at the amusement park, are not small matters. Our true values are communicated to our children during these exchanges.

As a school principal, I have seen the principle of sowing and reaping at work in families. Invariably, if a parent has a character issue, which they either tolerate or refuse to address, it will show up in the child. "In the Jewish tradition, the first step in repentance is *hakarat hachet*, recognizing the sin one has committed" (Telushkin, 151).

If we refuse to acknowledge our character deficiency, we can hardly expect our children to do so. Without repentance one will not grow in godly character. David repented for his sin: "David said to Natan, 'I have sinned against ADONAI'" (2 Sam. 12:13). "But David's response was different from Adam's, Eve's, Cain's, and Saul's; he admitted his guilt . . . . God, presumably delighted that finally a human being had owned up to his evil, instructed Nathan to tell David that his punishment would now be less severe" (Telushkin, 151–52). Being good examples to our children means repenting of our own sin.

Being Transparent With Our Children

We also need to be transparent with our children about our faults. It is important not to put on a pretense of perfection before our children. When we deal with sin honestly, including apologizing to our children when necessary, we demonstrate the reality of God in our lives. Our children are then able to see that walking according to God's Word makes a difference.

Rabbi Joseph Telushkin emphasizes, "What an awful message parents who never apologize send their children: 'You don't have to seek forgiveness when you mistreat someone weaker than yourself.' Or, 'because I raise and support you, I can treat you as I want. I don't have to say, 'I'm sorry,' even when I'm wrong'" (465). I have often had to apologize to my children. When we take the time to communicate with our children by confessing our wrong and seeking their forgiveness, we become a positive example to them.

Making Family Life Our Priority

1 Timothy 3:4–5 emphasizes the importance of prioritizing our family, especially for those in congregational leadership. The congregational leader "must manage his own household well, having children who obey him with all proper respect; for if a man can't manage his own household, how will he be able to care for God's Messianic Community?" In other words, watching over our family is essential before we attempt to manage a congregation.

Our family needs to be a priority instead of a sidelight; it should be the focus of our lives. Proverbs 27:23 says, "Take care to know the condition of your flocks." In twenty years as an educator, I cannot tell you how many times I have been surprised to find that parents do not really know what is going on in their teenager's life.

If we truly value family life, we will take concrete steps to show this in our daily schedule. Because we trust that God will provide everything we need as we seek first his Kingdom and righteousness, we should keep our work confined to reasonable hours. Although there may be periods when our jobs require extra time, we should not allow ourselves to fall into a habit of letting our work dominate our life to our family's detriment. We can make a commitment to be with our family for dinner in order to ensure a daily time of togetherness.

As the priest of the home, the father needs to know the condition of his "flock," his family. Unfortunately, many fathers "have become so wrapped up in the world that they have neglected their highest calling, the spiritual development of their children" (Meier, 92).

Love in Our Home

As a father, I need to continually remind myself to give my children hugs and kisses. Tickling them, dancing with them, and wrestling with them every day helps to strengthen our bond. We need to share healthy doses of love with our kids each day.

Rabbi Hayim Halevy Donin emphasizes the importance of physical contact with our children to express our love:

> Physical contact helps convey the message of love. The mother who embraces her infant and the father who cuddles his child provide the child with nourishment as vital as milk. Milk nourishes the body; signs of affection nourish the soul. Both are equally necessary to sound health; the deprivation of either can be harmful to normal growth and development. Parents should, therefore, not hesitate to physically embrace their children, to give them hugs, plant kisses, place affectionate pats on their heads, and hold their hands. Such physical contacts, made spontaneously and for no special reason, speak louder than words and contribute to a warm feeling of being loved. (Donin, 64–65)

Biblical Communication

James 1:19–20 provides us with important principles of communication: "Let every person be quick to listen but slow to speak, slow to get angry; for a person's anger does not accomplish God's righteousness!" We need to be quick to listen to our children:

> Remember that listening involves shutting the mouth. When seeking to communicate, create a non-threatening climate and avoid non-verbal gestures that communicate negativity and threaten the other person, your spouse or child. Empathize, don't sympathize. Seek to understand feelings rather than words. Ask questions for clarification. Use positive words: "You mean . . ." but do not use, "You

don't mean . . ." (Switzer and Switzer, "Parenting Is an Adventure Seminar," 89)

In addition to being "quick to listen," we should be "slow to speak." Proverbs 18:13 says, "To answer someone before hearing him out is both stupid and embarrassing." Parents should patiently listen to their children and avoid interrupting them before they can share what is on their heart. For me, it is sometimes difficult to stop and listen when my children argue with each other. I want to jump in there and admonish them, but I have to remind myself to hear both sides before I decide how to proceed.

Finally, we should be "slow to get angry." Proverbs 17:27 says, "A knowledgeable person controls his tongue; a discerning person controls his temper." When we repeat our teenager's point of view in our own words, we show understanding. Proverbs 15:1 says, "A gentle response deflects fury, but a harsh word makes tempers rise." Simply responding with a soft answer can defuse much anger from our children.

There are no magical formulas for communicating with our children. Patience, hearing out our young people, avoiding harsh reactions, being real with our children (avoiding hypocrisy), and making wise judgments are all principles of biblical communication. Sometimes we may feel like judges in a courtroom deciding the tough cases that our children bring us, particularly with respect to sibling conflict. We may have to communicate one value to one child while communicating a different value to another. James 3:17–18 counsels us to be peacemakers: "But the wisdom from above is, first of all, pure, then peaceful, kind, open to reason, full of mercy and good fruits, without partiality and without hypocrisy. And peacemakers who sow seed in peace raise a harvest of righteousness."

Love's Connection to Discipline

Love alone should motivate us to discipline our children. Love looks to the long-term interests of our children; it desires to see them blessed. Hebrews 12:5–8 explains that discipline is an expression of God's fatherly love:

> And you have forgotten that word of encouragement that addresses you as sons:
>   My son, do not make light of the Lord's discipline, and do not lose heart when he rebukes you, because the Lord disciplines those he loves, and he punishes everyone he accepts as a son. Endure hardship as discipline; God is treating you as sons. For what son is not disciplined by his father? If you are not disciplined (and everyone undergoes discipline), then you are illegitimate children and not true sons.

Although children will rarely express appreciation while they are undergoing discipline, they do gain a sense of security and care from us when we consistently apply godly discipline. Furthermore, children respect us for disciplining them:

> Moreover, we have all had human fathers who disciplined us and we respected them for it. How much more should we submit to the Father of our spirits and live! Our fathers disciplined us for a little while as they thought best; but God disciplines us for our good, that we may share in his holiness. No discipline seems pleasant at the time, but painful. Later on, however, it produces a harvest of righteousness and peace for those who have been trained by it. (Heb. 12:9–11)

Noticing the Difference

Through following biblical principles, a family may be different enough that children notice and ask a critical question: "Why?" God anticipated this:

> Some day your child will ask you, "What is the meaning of the instructions, laws and rulings which ADONAI our God

has laid down for you?" Then you will tell your child, "We were slaves to Pharaoh in Egypt, and ADONAI brought us out of Egypt with a strong hand." (Deut. 6:20–21; cf. Exod. 12:25–27)

One way our children can see their family stand out from the larger society is by how we dress. Very early in life our kids will be able to notice differences in dress and we ought not miss this opportunity to teach them. As we know, the prevailing trends in dress have descended to a very low standard. We need to hold the line in this area, even if it seems there are no modest styles of clothing available in stores.

Instead of ignoring the issue of dress and giving into the prevailing culture, we can help our young people see that our families are different. Rabbi Simcha Bunim Cohen writes, "The Poskim teach us that the sanctity of the home is primarily maintained through the laws of *tznius* [modesty]. Tznius creates an atmosphere of holiness and wholesomeness that permeates family life" (30). We can help our daughters and sons understand that much is communicated to others about ourselves simply by the way we dress.

When my brothers and I saw neighborhood friends and peers in our congregation involved in ungodly activities, my parents helped us understand in a positive way that our family was different, and that was OK! We should use the times when our children notice family differences as prime teachable moments to help them strengthen convictions.

Dealing With Winning and Losing

Another way to be good role models is to have a godly approach to winning and losing, particularly in competitions. This is important for young children as they begin playing Little League baseball, soccer, basketball, and other competitive sports.

Unfortunately, too often parents try to live vicariously through their kids and attempt to compensate for a perceived lack in their own lives. If parents are not careful, they can unknowingly place undue pressure on their children to achieve, when what their children really need is to have a positive, enjoyable experience.

One way to provide children with a healthy, character-building experience while playing on a sports team is to be sure that our own attitude toward winning is a healthy one. If we see ourselves as a success or a failure based on the outcomes in our life, then that value will be conveyed to our children. Consequently, when our child is not on the winning team, he may automatically see himself as a failure. No matter how well the child has played, he may break down emotionally because he lost. The focus should rather be on the process: "The Torah value is indeed that it is the process rather than the conclusion that counts. All a person can do is the best he can do under given circumstances. . . . A person cannot control outcome" (Twerski and Schwartz, 75). "ADONAI doesn't see the way humans see–humans look at the outward appearance, but ADONAI looks at the heart" (1 Sam. 16:7).

Yeshua himself said, "Stop judging by surface appearances, and judge the right way!" (John 7:24). We need to avoid the tendency to make judgments based on external outcomes. I have coached games in which my team played heroically and passionately and yet lost, as well as games in which we scored a blowout victory and yet didn't play to the best of our ability. If we want our children to have a positive experience, then it is up to us to help them have the right perspective.

Colossians 3:23 says, "Whatever you do, work at it with all your heart, as working for the Lord, not for men." We want our children to have a wholehearted work ethic for Yeshua. We desire that they would seek to please him with their words, actions, and heart motivations rather than living under some false pressure to succeed. If we approach sports in this way, then sports can be a tool to build godly character in our children.

The Calling of Parents

Paul urged, "Run in such a way as to get the prize" (1 Cor. 9:24). Parents have a huge opportunity to positively influence their children through their daily example. Children will catch much more from our lives than from our words.

One day as my seven-year-old son was waiting for me in my office after soccer practice, he noticed a poster with the words of 1 Chronicles 4:10 on it: "Please bless me by enlarging my territory. May your hand be with me! Keep me from harm, so that it will not cause me pain." I told him that I pray that prayer daily. Caleb then prayed that God would help him obey his parents with a good attitude. After he came home, Silvia complimented him in the afternoon and then later that evening for his obedience and positive attitude. After receiving the second compliment, our son told his mother that he had prayed and asked God to help him obey his parents with a good attitude. Caleb saw that God answered his prayer! When our children see God working in our lives, they can follow that example and experience God working in their lives.

Psalm 127:3 says that "children [are] a reward from" the Lord. The reward for embracing God's calling to parent is very great indeed. It is much greater than a job promotion, a hefty salary raise, a new car, or a beautiful house. When we parent our children for the Lord, we are storing up treasure in heaven and doing work that will last for eternity.

Chapter Four

A Vision for Each Child

ANY PARENT with more than one child sees the God-given differences in their children. Studying our children to understand their motivational bents, talents, strengths, and weaknesses enables us to steer them in the direction best suited for them. Providing them with many different kinds of opportunities helps them to discover personal areas of interest and gifting.

The Prophetic Meaning of a Name

The Scriptures indicate that a name can speak of a child's identity and future. Matthew 1:21 says, "She will give birth to a son, and you are to name him Yeshua, because he will save his people from their sins." Luke 1:13–17 speaks of the prophetic implications of John's name:

> But the angel said to him: "Do not be afraid, Zechariah; your prayer has been heard. Your wife Elizabeth will bear you a son, and you are to give him the name John. He will be a joy and delight to you, and many will rejoice because of his birth, for he will be great in the sight of the Lord. He

is never to take wine or other fermented drink, and he will be filled with the Holy Spirit even from birth. Many of the people of Israel will he bring back to the Lord their God. And he will go on before the Lord, in the spirit and power of Elijah, to turn the hearts of the fathers to their children and the disobedient to the wisdom of the righteous–to make ready a people prepared for the Lord."

Because Zechariah did not believe the angel's words, he became mute. When Zechariah named his child "Yochanan" (John), his speech returned to him.

God uses names many times in his Word to communicate messages to his people. Sometimes he changes names, such as Abram to Abraham and Jacob to Israel. Isaiah says that his children "are signs and symbols in Israel from the Lord Almighty" (Isa. 8:18). Their names have prophetic meaning.

Likewise, the name that we choose for our child is very important to God. We should keep this in mind when we are contemplating a name. We should ask God for guidance. We can study Scripture for meanings of names and what each person stood for as he or she followed God. The meaning of that name and the spiritual principles that go along with the name can be communicated to our child over and over as he or she grows up.

My son Caleb knows very well that he is named after one of the two Israeli spies that stood with God and proclaimed to the Jewish people that they could take the Promised Land. The need to walk in biblical courage as expressed in Joshua 1:9 has been ingrained in his spirit: "Haven't I ordered you, 'Be strong, be bold'? So don't be afraid or downhearted, because ADONAI your God is with you wherever you go." It was a source of joy for my wife, Silvia, to overhear Caleb one day encouraging his three-year-old brother who was afraid to go down the stairs in the dark. As Caleb helped him down the steps, he quoted from Joshua 1:9 and told Nehemiah not to be afraid, that he could do it! Your child's name can be a source of blessing and godly character as he embraces the identity of his name.

I enjoy using nicknames that are connected to the meanings of my kids' names. For instance, I like to call my son, "Champ Caleb," to encourage him to be a courageous champion who will take the "promised land" God has for him. My son Nehemiah likes to build things, so I gave him the nickname "Nehemiah the Builder," making the connection to Nehemiah who was led by God to rebuild the walls of Jerusalem.

Even though our children may not presently be walking according to the meaning of their name, we can speak the power of their names into their lives. Names can be prophetic in nature. They can have meaning and speak of the child's identity in the Lord.

Process Objectives in Training the Child

Luke wrote about Yeshua at age twelve: "And Yeshua grew both in wisdom and in stature, gaining favor both with other people and with God" (Luke 2:52). A similar statement is made about the boy Samuel: "And the boy Samuel continued to grow in stature and in favor with the Lord and with men" (I Samuel 2:26). Four process objectives that we should have when training our children are wisdom, stature, favor with God, and favor with others.

Growth in Wisdom

Our children need to grow in wisdom. They need to know what is right and true. It is notable that many biblical proverbs begin with the words, "My son":

> My son, if you will receive my words
> and store my commands inside you,
> paying attention to wisdom
> inclining your mind toward understanding –
> yes, if you will call for insight
> and raise your voice for discernment,
> if you seek it as you would silver
> and search for it as for hidden treasure –
> then you will understand the fear of ADONAI
> and find knowledge of God. (Prov. 2:1–5)

Growth in Stature

Children also need to grow in stature. They need to be nurtured physically. Too many children in our society are, quite frankly, malnourished. Too often their diets consist of candy and things that "taste good" instead of what is healthy for them.

Helping our children be good stewards of their bodies is critical to their growth: "Don't you know that you people are God's temple and that God's Spirit lives in you? So if anyone destroys God's temple, God will destroy him. For God's temple is holy, and you yourselves are that temple" (1 Cor. 3:16–17). Our bodies are temples of the Holy Spirit; indeed, God resides within us. Healthy recreation, proper diet, and sufficient sleep are very important to one's personal growth.

Children's recreation too often consists of stationary activities, such as watching television or playing video games. David Walsh, in an address entitled "Educating Children in the Dot-Com Age," provided the following statistics of children's average weekly use of time: alone with father, half an hour; alone with mother, two and a half hours; doing homework, a little over two hours; doing non-school reading, half an hour; playing computer video games, seven hours; and watching television, twenty-five hours. While we could draw various conclusions from these statistics, we can see the prodigious amount of time being spent doing things that contribute to the mind's virtual reality as opposed to healthy physical exercise and play.

Children need to get outside and participate in sports and other activities. They need to be fit and active. A farm is a great place to grow up with daily chores required of everyone in the family. In the absence of that, children still need regular activities that require physical exertion, such as household chores, newspaper routes, or simply playing outside.

Growth in Favor With God

Children also need to grow in favor with God. They need to experience the love of God. God's grace toward them is his unmerited favor and empowerment; good works cannot earn God's favor.

As our children embrace this kind of relationship, they will grow secure in the love of God. Developing favor with God leads to success in every area of our life.

Growth in Favor With Others

Finally, children need to grow in favor with other people. Whether it is their parents, their teachers, their classmates, their neighbors, their teammates, or their coaches, their life and response to others should engender favor. Training our children in relational skills such as greeting others, making eye contact, listening attentively, asking questions, and simply living right will naturally result in favor with others.

Rather than fighting back or running away when faced with conflict, our children can learn to stand in these situations and positively influence those around them in the ways of the Lord. They can learn to walk in godly courage because of the Lord's presence with them: "Have I not commanded you? Be strong and courageous. Do not be terrified; do not be discouraged, for the Lord your God will be with you wherever you go" (Josh. 1:9).

These process objectives–wisdom, stature, favor with God, and favor with others–cannot be compartmentalized. Growth in these objectives occurs concurrently; our children will not excel in one without improvement in the others. If mediocrity is allowed in one area, eventually that condition will impact growth in the other areas. However, as our children grow in the Lord, they will experience accomplishment in all of these areas.

Children intrinsically desire to please their parents. We should therefore develop a repertoire of praise for our children. If we praise them for outward expressions, such as their good looks, they will emphasize those areas in their growth. When our children receive an "A" in school, Silvia and I are careful to praise them for their hard work and diligent study, not simply for the fact that they received an "A." If we focus on praising our children for growth in their character, then they will understand that their character is most important.

A Distinct Purpose From God

Parents who have a vision for their children know that God created them with specific purposes in mind. I can attest that I have been impacted by my mother speaking over me the words of Jeremiah 29:11: "'For I know what plans I have in mind for you,' says ADONAI, 'plans for well-being, not for bad things; so that you can have hope and a future.'" My mother taught me that God had a special plan for my life, and that God was doing something great through me for his Kingdom.

We need to build high expectations in young children concerning God's destiny for their lives. Instead of asking them, "What do you want to be when you grow up?", we can ask them questions such as, "What do you think might be the Lord's purpose for your life?" We can steer our children in the way they should go, as we understand how God has uniquely made them. Let them know that God has a very special plan for them. Referring to Proverbs 22:6, Donin emphasizes, "The most lasting results come from recognizing personality differences, different levels of ability, and varying interests. Each child is a unique work of art, to be appreciated, loved, and enjoyed for himself" (64). Psalm 127:4 says, "The children born when one is young, are like arrows in the hand of a warrior." God can use us as expert archers to point our children in the right direction, with the ultimate aim of hitting the bull's eye for God's Kingdom.

Chapter Five

Respecting Authority

SADLY, MANY PEOPLE HAVE LOST RESPECT for authority. Even our bumper stickers have messages like "Question Authority." I heard an experienced administrator from a religious school once say that fifteen years ago he would make a decision, the child would then go home and communicate with his parent, and later he would get a call from the parent, saying, in effect, "My child tells me this; I want to know what the truth is." Now, however, too often the scenario is like this: the child goes home, gives a report, and then the administrator gets a call from the parent saying, "My child tells me this, and I am so disappointed in how you handled it." All too often, parents judge the matter before speaking with the teacher.

One can easily see the breakdown that has occurred in our society's view of authority. Unfortunately, this view has had an impact on parents. Biblical principles of authority are critical for us to understand and embrace if we are going to successfully train and discipline our children.

God's Authority

God is the ultimate authority. Psalm 47:2 refers to God as, "The Lord Most High, the great King over all the earth!" There is no authority above God and his reign will never end, as King Nebuchadnezzar learned:

> I blessed the Most High, I praised and gave honor to him who lives forever. For his rulership is everlasting, his kingdom endures through all generations. All who live on earth are counted as nothing. He does what he wishes with the army of heaven and with those living on earth. No one can hold back his hand or ask him, "What are you doing?" (Dan. 4:34–35)

According to the Scriptures, everyone is under authority. There is no president, king, or terrorist who is not under authority. Ultimately, everyone must answer to the Authority of the universe. When we place ourselves squarely under God's authority, we can walk securely in our parental authority in a way that brings blessing to our children.

God-Given Parental Authority

Romans 13:1 says, "Everyone is to obey the governing authorities. For there is no authority that is not from God, and the existing authorities have been placed where they are by God." God has given parents authority in the family.

The Scriptures provide boundaries for the family. For example, parents do not have the right to tell their children to break God's laws. The institution of the family is for the well being of our children.

Parental Prerogatives

Colossians 3:20 provides a clear directive to children: "Children, obey your parents in everything; for this pleases the Lord." Our children are required to do what we tell them to do. In our society today, this may sound extreme; however, parents have prerogatives to fulfill God-given responsibilities.

I recall when Anna was only sixteen months old and showing the strength of her own will. Silvia and I had to set our faces "like a flint" to lovingly discipline her so that one day she would be an instrument of God. The motivation for us to use our God-given rights to require our children's obedience is the firm hope in God that they will one day internalize his Word.

We must take these rights seriously in order for us to fulfill our parental responsibility. We are accountable for our children's actions. God gave us this job knowing that we're not perfect; yet, he still entrusted us with this task.

The Child's Understanding of God's Authority

Our children will respond to God's authority based on how they have been brought up to respond to their parents' authority. Psalm 15:4 commends the person "who keeps his oath even when it hurts." It is important for us to keep our word to our children so that they learn that God keeps his Word to them. Before our children reach kindergarten, we should train them to submit to our authority so that they will be ready to submit to other authorities that we place over them, especially their teachers.

Our word to our children is critical. When we say that we are going to do something, they expect we will do it. When Caleb was two-years old, I put him to bed one evening when my wife was out. I told him that Mommy would give him a hug when she came home. When Silvia returned, I asked her to give Caleb a hug because I had told him she would. Silvia thought that he might be asleep. However, she went up and sure enough, he was sitting there, waiting for her in his crib. When he noticed his mom, he stood up and said, "Hug, hug!" Silvia asked Caleb if he had been waiting for her. He said, "Yes." She asked if he had been sleeping or had been awake. He had been awake. She then gave him a big hug. The fact that Caleb was patiently sitting in his crib shows that he felt we were worthy of his trust. I hope that we will continue to be trustworthy.

Keeping our word also relates to how our children will view the Scriptures. When we make idle threats without requiring our children's obedience, they are being trained not to respond to direction. God does not make idle threats. He does what he says. Although no parent is perfect, the consistency with which we keep our word directly affects our children's ability to trust God's Word.

Maintaining Respect for Authorities

It is very important that we respect authority. Parents should reserve judgment about anything their child says concerning a teacher until after they talk with the teacher. Often a child's report reflects limited understanding. In my experience as a parent, teacher, and principal, simply communicating with the teacher makes the difference. The main reason, however, for reserving judgment until we talk with the teacher is to teach our children to respect authority.

When we express disrespect for an authority, we are giving our children license to do the same. We may disagree with a particular decision made by an authority but we must still abide by it.

As a glaring example of how parents can violate this principle, consider the treatment of umpires at Little League baseball games. Parents often get caught up in the game and berate the umpire for his calls. When parents do this, they are setting themselves up for their children to show disrespect for their own authority. Umpires, like all people, make mistakes. Parents should help their children understand that umpires provide secure boundaries to enable everyone to enjoy the game.

One of my daily prayers for my children is that they would obey their parents, teachers, and coaches. I want them to grow up with a heartfelt commitment to live under authority. As we maintain respect for authorities, even when we disagree with them, we help our children learn to respect authority. This, in turn, bolsters their respect for our authority.

Chapter Six

Using Our Authority

J OHN 1:1–4 explains that Yeshua is the author of life: "In the beginning was the Word, and the Word was with God, and the Word was God. He was with God in the beginning. All things came to be through him, and without him nothing made had being. In him was life, and the life was the light of mankind."

The Gospels tell us, "They were amazed at the way he taught, for he did not instruct them like the Torah-teachers, but as one who had authority himself" (Mark 1:22). Yeshua is the Author and has authority over all things. As Yeshua was commissioning his disciples, he told them, "All authority in heaven and on earth has been given to me. Therefore go and make disciples of all nations...teaching them to obey everything I have commanded you" (Matt. 28:18–20).

We have been given the authority to author life in our first disciples, our children. When one of my boys was five months old, my wife and I saw the life-authoring impact I had on him. I had to go away for a conference; it was the first time that I was away from him for more than a day. Normally a very calm and happy baby, he became very fussy and cried whenever Silvia laid him down for a nap. Ordinarily he would sleep peacefully, but on this day he needed to be held. Well, my wife and I wondered whether our baby was missing me. After I returned home and played with him, he returned to being his happy and content self again. We can never underestimate the capacity that we have to author life in our children.

If we accept this commission to train our children, we can rely on the authority of Yeshua. We have the authority to build up, to correct, to rebuke, to encourage, and to make disciples of our children.

Using Authority Versus Being Authoritarian

The Lord calls us to walk in our God-given authority without being authoritarian. While parents should require their children's obedience and not abdicate their rightful role, true biblical authority is not dictatorial. Colossians 3:21 tells fathers to "not embitter your children, or they will become discouraged." Ephesians 6:4 tells fathers to "not exasperate your children." It is critical that we exercise calm authority without being harsh.

1 Corinthians 10:13 says that God gives us a way of escape when dealing with temptation. We can show our children a way out when they may be tempted to disobey us. One thing that I like to do is give my children a "two-minute notice." When our children are absorbed in an activity, perhaps playing with a toy or immersed in a computer game, a two-minute notice helps them to prepare for the end of that activity before they are told to "come to dinner."

Gary and Anne Marie Ezzo, the directors of Growing Families International, advocate "the appeal process" as a tool that enables parents not to exasperate their children. When we give a command, only two responses are acceptable: "Yes, Mommy or Daddy," or "May I appeal?" In order for the appeal process to work, the child needs to be generally obedient. The child should ask for the appeal in a humble manner. If the parent agrees to the appeal, the child is to provide the parent with information he is unaware of. The child understands that the parent may respond to the appeal with "Yes," "No," or "Maybe." If the parent denies the appeal, the child is not to continue to beg for his way. Only one appeal can be made (Ezzo and Ezzo, 281-287).

My son Caleb has mastered the appeal process. Sometimes after dinner, I am in a hurry to get the dishes going. Caleb's job is to put the dishes in the dishwasher. I might say to the children, "Let's get after the dishes." Caleb often has said, "May I appeal?" After I agree to his appeal, he says, "I'm still eating." Of course, I normally let him finish.

Avoidance of Shaming Our Children

Sometimes parents will shame their children as a misguided means of controlling them. Far from being a life-giving approach, this strategy only builds resentment in them. While we do need to address our children's sin, we also need to value their feelings and emotions. We need to bring sin into the light without heaping condemnation on them.

Not shaming children applies particularly to public situations:

> Never embarrass a child before others, not in front of your
> friends and certainly not in front of his. Even when you
> justifiably rebuke a child for some misdeed or error, and
> the child knows that he deserves it, the rebuke ought not
> to be made in the presence of others. Holding a child up to
> public scorn only builds up the kind of resentment, which,
> if allowed to accumulate and fester, may someday lash out
> in open rebelliousness and defiance. (Donin, 70)

There may be times when a child has committed a public offense. In this situation, it is advisable that our rebuke occur in a private manner, away from the spotlight, away from the group. This way our child's personal dignity is preserved. We can rebuke a child privately and, if necessary, then have the child make an apology before the group.

When we do "blow up" and are harsh with our children, we need to acknowledge our wrong and seek their forgiveness. As a father, I have apologized many times to my children for speaking harshly to them. Sometimes we will miss the mark, but it is important that we avoid bringing our children to that point of being bitter, discouraged, or exasperated.

Biblical authority is not dictatorial. Speaking with a harsh tone, using peremptory commands, and expressing frustration should not be our usual method. Rather, God calls us to walk in authority that is servant-like: "Shepherd the flock of God that is in your care, exercising oversight not out of constraint, but willingly, as God wants . . . with enthusiasm; also not as *machers* [big shots] domineering over those in your care, but as people who become examples to the flock" (1 Pet. 5:2–3).

As we serve our family, carefully watching over our "flock" with enthusiasm and a positive example, we will be exercising our authority in a way that brings life to our children. Instead of constantly seeking short-term compliance through a dictatorial style, we need to trust God for the long-term results. As we exercise authority and require our children's obedience in a way that honors the Lord, we will eventually see good fruit in our children's lives.

The Centurion's Understanding of Authority

When the centurion heard that Yeshua was coming to his house to heal his servant, he sent friends to give Yeshua this message:

> Sir, don't trouble yourself. I'm not worthy to have you come under my roof. This is why I didn't presume to approach you myself. Instead, just give a command and let my servant recover. For I too am a man set under authority. I have soldiers under me; and I say to this one, "Go!" and he goes; and to another, "Come!" and he comes. (Luke 7:6–8)

Yeshua was amazed at the centurion's faith. The centurion understood what it meant to walk under authority. Because he himself was a man "under authority," he understood the spiritual dynamic of leading by example: he could not expect those under him to obey him if he did not obey his superiors.

We will have much more confidence requiring our children to obey us if we are walking in full-hearted obedience to the Lord.

We will have moral authority if we respect authorities in our lives and in our children's lives, including elders, teachers, coaches, employers, the police, and the justice system.

Finally, the centurion understood that Yeshua had authority over all things, including health and sickness. He told Yeshua to "just give a command and let my servant recover." As we authoritatively speak words of faith over our children, we will see God's order and authority come into their lives.

The Principle of Unity

Unity between father and mother enables parents to more effectively author life in their children (cf. Ps. 133). The two major authority figures in children's lives are their father and mother. When parents exercise authority in a unified and biblical manner, God grants long-term blessing and life to children. Sometimes if children do not get their way with one parent, they will pursue the other. This should not be allowed. If one parent provides direction, that should be accepted by the child. Any disagreements that parents have should be worked out in private; our children need to know that we are solidly unified in our standards and expectations for our children.

In the school setting, I have seen students try to work a parent against a teacher or vice versa, especially when they are being held accountable for their actions. Children will try to wriggle free from personal responsibility. However, as the parents and teacher stay unified, the child's disciplinary issues can be successfully addressed. The child's long-term character is strengthened. Without proper respect for authority, a child will not be able to learn. The ability of our children to listen to and obey their teachers will greatly impact the effectiveness of their education. Parents and teachers must stick together.

The Scriptures tell us that God's word will not return void but will fulfill its purpose (Isa. 55:11). Parents need to work together to author life in their children. By instructing our children in God's Word and speaking Scriptures over them, we help them to see themselves from God's perspective; we build them up in the Lord.

Chapter Seven

Declaring the Victory of Messiah

BELIEVERS KNOW THAT YESHUA has already won the victory for us through his death and resurrection. However, amid the daily pressures of life, we can forget this fundamental spiritual triumph. Even more so, as we train our children through all of the struggles they endure, it is easy to get discouraged and wonder if we will ever "get the victory." God wants us to raise our young people with the understanding and vision that they are victorious in Messiah. The way we do this is to continually declare the truths of God's Word in their lives.

Speaking Words of Life

When we speak the Word of God over our children, a living faith is developed within them. As Romans 10:17 tells us, "So trust comes from what is heard, and what is heard comes through a word proclaimed about the Messiah." We need to actively declare the living Word over our children so that they constantly hear it. Children are naturally trusting. They believe what we say!

The story of God's call of Moses is instructive. This great leader, who grew up without a godly father, had quite an inauspicious start. Moses told God, "Who am I . . .?" (Exod. 3:11) and "Oh, ADONAI, I'm a terrible speaker. I always have been, and I'm no better now, even after you've spoken to your servant! My words come slowly, my tongue moves slowly" (Exod. 4:10). Perhaps because Moses did not have a godly father figure to encourage him, he initially had a very difficult time seeing himself from God's perspective.

Silvia and I discovered early on that one of our sons, like Moses, had a speech challenge. We immediately chose to believe that God would turn that challenge around for his glory, and we committed to speaking positive words of life over our son's speech. Since then, we have seen our son embrace his speech therapy; he is very motivated to improve his speech. As our young people mature, our challenge is to speak words of life that help them to grow up with the inner confidence that God has for them.

Praying Over Our Children

The Aaronic blessing is a God-given prayer that we can regularly speak over our children:

> May ADONAI bless you and keep you. May ADONAI make his face shine on you and show you his favor. May ADONAI lift up his face toward you and give you peace. (Num. 6:24–26)

This is a prayer of blessing, that God will watch over our children, go before them, show them his favor, and give them his peace. What more could we want?

When we pray, our children learn to respond to life's challenges with prayer. When our daughter was almost two years old, and Silvia was pregnant with our second child, a somewhat humorous incident occurred. Anna noticed holes in her mother's socks and said, "Oh no, holes!" She then asked, "Pray?" Then, she went up to her mommy, sat next to her on the couch, and bowed her head.

Then Anna prayed, "Jesus, baby, pray." After her mother excitedly thanked her, she laid her hand on her mother's chest and prayed, "Jesus, baby, pray." Other than saying "amen," that was the first time our daughter had prayed aloud, and she did so on her own. She was motivated to pray over her sibling in her mother's womb just as she had seen her parents praying over her and her soon-to-be-arriving brother.

We need to bless our children continually. In their presence, we should regularly pray God's blessings over them: that they are blessed with every spiritual blessing in Messiah, that God always causes them to triumph in Messiah, that they are more than conquerors in Messiah, that they are blessed so they can be a blessing to others, and that God is with them.

When we respond to life's challenges by praying, we are communicating that our response to difficulty is not discouragement and defeat, but rather hope and victory. Philippians 4:6–7 says, "Don't worry about anything; on the contrary, make your requests known to God by prayer and petition, with thanksgiving. Then God's *shalom*, passing all understanding, will keep your hearts and minds safe in union with the Messiah Yeshua." We need to share with our children the simple answers to our prayers. My wife recalls our baby Joshua being fussy; she prayed for him, and he calmed down. When we shared this testimony with the family, Anna was overjoyed!

Let young people see that when we are tempted to worry, we pray instead. When we are tempted to complain, we give sincere thanks for our lot in life, instead. When we are tempted to be resentful, wallow in self-pity, or criticize others, we practice forgiveness and prayer.

When I was on a trip out of town, my credit card information was stolen. The perpetrator bought a number of expensive items within a few days. Well, Silvia particularly felt that we had been violated and expressed anger towards the person. However, she saw our children picking up the offense. She realized that we needed to forgive the person. So we gathered our family together, prayed, and forgave the person as a family.

When we pray with our children about life's challenges, the Lord opens their hearts and can work in them in such a way that they are washed from sin and the cares of this world. As they are cleansed in their inner being, they are able to continue forward in a positive framework with renewed motivation to live for God.

Winning the Prize

Philippians 3:13–14 encourages us:

> Brothers, I, for my part, do not think of myself as having yet gotten hold of it; but one thing I do: forgetting what is behind me and straining forward toward what lies ahead, I keep pursuing the goal in order to win the prize offered by God's upward calling in the Messiah Yeshua.

God is interested in how our families run the race. He calls us to run this race so that we win his eternal prize in Messiah! For us, that means we need to pay the price of training our children, for without training we cannot expect children to be prepared to run the race so that they will win their eternal reward. Often, the price of training is investing the time to speak God's perspective into our children as they confront life issues. We need to help them forget past failures as they walk in the cleansing power of confessed sin. As we do, we are helping them to be committed to excellence as opposed to perfection. Excellence is an outstanding motivator with an orientation toward our children's future; by contrast, perfectionism can cause them to focus on past failures and be hesitant to take on future challenges.

One of my continuing challenges with my own children is helping them to see that I simply want them to live, work, and play wholeheartedly for Yeshua. If they do not get an "A" on a test or if they fail to win a soccer game, that's okay. God is more concerned with the process of what they are doing. They can control their effort, such as their study habits, but they need to leave the results in the Lord's hands.

We need to walk this out in our own lives if we expect children to have a healthy perspective. They need to see us working with all of our heart for the Lord (Col. 3:23). If we fail to win a certain job contract, our children need to see that we can give it to the Lord and move on with a positive focus instead of wallowing in defeat and self-pity. If we walk in this way, we will be teaching our children how to deal with failure in a healthy way and to move forward to the next challenge with a victorious attitude.

Walking by Faith

God calls us to walk by faith, not by feelings. I recall talking to a young man about his words when he gets up in the morning. I challenged him to avoid saying things like "I'm tired . . . I don't feel good . . . I don't want to go to school." Instead, I encouraged him to speak words of life, such as, "This is the day the Lord has made; I'm going to rejoice and be glad in it!"

Proverbs 18:21 says, "The tongue has the power of life and death." The words we speak will impact our lives tremendously. In fact, if we use our words in a life-giving way, the Scriptures says that we will shine like stars in this world (Phil. 2:14–16). Parents, if you want your children to show forth Yeshua's light to others, teach them to walk in contentment, without arguing and complaining.

My nine-year old daughter received a fine compliment once. Her aunt noticed that she not only obeyed consistently, but that she also obeyed with a good attitude when doing activities that were not her preference. When our children conduct their lives without arguing about their preferences or complaining about their lot, others see that the Lord is making a difference in their lives. That is a powerful testimony!

If our children live by their feelings, their lives will be like a roller coaster, up and down and every which way. However, if our children are trained to live by faith in God's Word, they will learn to walk out the promises of God for their life. Their faith will produce faithfulness, which will in turn be used by God to develop Messiah-like character within them.

As our young people learn to entrust their lives to the Lord, they will understand their identity in Messiah and God's victorious plan for their lives. As they walk in faith, they will see themselves increasingly as "aliens and temporary residents" (1 Pet. 2:11) who are simply passing through a foreign land while on this earth. This faith perspective will enable them to not be swayed by momentary troubles and circumstances; they will walk with confidence.

The Word of Their Testimony

We need to teach our children God's strategy for victorious overcoming, as described in Revelation 12:10–11:

> Now have come God's victory, power and kingship, and the authority of his Messiah; because the Accuser of our brothers, who accuses them day and night before God, has been thrown out! *They defeated him because of the Lamb's blood and because of the message of their witness.* Even when facing death they did not cling to life. (italics added)

Children learn to be overcomers in life as they choose to trust God's Word instead of believing the lies of the enemy. We need to take the time to teach our children how to apply the blood of the Lamb to their hearts through repentance and confession of sin. We can encourage them to walk in faith by remembering that they are disciples of Yeshua. As they learn to affirm the victory of God in their lives, and as they begin to understand that God has bought them with a price, they will develop a faith that will enable them to love God more than their own lives. Satan's accusations will have no impact on them. They will understand and walk out their glorious position in Messiah.

Learning to overcome is a process. 1 John 2:14 says, "You young people, I have written you because you are strong–the Word of God remains in you, and you have overcome the Evil One." When I was a college student, I recall a season when my life was hanging in the balance. In order to maintain a sense of spiritual life, I searched the Scriptures, determined to praise God despite doubt, and confessed biblical truths over my life. By the grace of God, the Lord helped me overcome my doubt because his Word became part of my very being.

In the life of a believer, the victory is won or lost in the mind:

> For although we do live in the world, we do not wage war
> in a worldly way, because the weapons we use to wage war
> are not worldly. On the contrary, they have God's power
> for demolishing strongholds. We demolish arguments and
> every arrogance that raises itself up against the knowledge
> of God; *we take every thought captive and make it obey the*
> *Messiah.* (2 Cor. 10:3–5, italics added)

We need to teach our children to take captive their thoughts
and to line them up with Messiah and his Word.

I often tell my kids to think about Yeshua when they are afraid.
At the age of six, one of my sons received a deep gash below his
knee while playing soccer. The blood was gushing out and he was
afraid. Once we got the blood under control, he started expressing
hysteria over having to go to the hospital to get stitches. I encouraged him to think about Yeshua, and his testimony is that God
helped him to be calm and at peace as the nurses and the doctors
did their job and stitched him up.

While it certainly was not a pleasant experience for my son,
he was able to learn a very important truth expressed in Isaiah
26:3: "You will keep in perfect peace him whose mind is stead-
fast, because he trusts in you." As he focused on God and God's
ways, my son walked in Yeshua's victory. Regular affirmations of
Yeshua's victory in their lives will help our children have a victorious attitude and grow to be champions of God.

Part Two

Practical Parenting Methods

T HE WAY WE GO about training our children will ultimately show our values to them. As James 2:18 says, "Show me this faith of yours without the actions, and I will show you my faith by my actions!" We show whether we are really committed to following God and his Word through our actions.

The number one goal of family life should be following the Messiah. Our daily example is of utmost importance. Is it one of integrity–a life in which our words and actions match up? Or do we send mixed messages to our children?

In order to communicate a clear standard, we must deal with our own sin issues. 1 John 1:7 says, "But if we are walking in the light, as he is in the light, then we have fellowship with each other, and the blood of his Son Yeshua purifies us from all sin." We need to be honest with children when we blow it. When I have had an argument with Silvia that has upset the peace of the home (and my children are aware of this fact), I go to my children, with my wife, and openly deal with that transgression.

As the Scripture above implies, if parents deny their sin to the family, the family will have no fellowship. However, as we acknowledge our own sin, the standard is reestablished and a sense of rightness is restored; then our family is able to have renewed fellowship. In addition to dealing with our own sin, we must seek to live by the power of the Spirit of God. Galatians 5:22–23 lists the characteristics of those who live by the Spirit's power: "But the fruit of the Spirit is love, joy, peace, patience, kindness, goodness, faithfulness, gentleness and self-control. Against such things there is no law."

It is within this framework that we will discuss how to make our children disciples of Yeshua. Matthew 28:19–20 commissions us to "go and make disciples of all nations . . . teaching them to obey everything I have commanded you." Discipleship begins in the family. In the next several chapters, we will look at what we should teach our children, setting boundaries, the nature of training, dealing with rebellion, relational communication, the *Sh'ma* as a teaching model, and what children can learn from the biblical festivals.

Chapter Eight

Content of Instruction

T HE GOAL OF OUR INSTRUCTION is for children to apply God's Word to every aspect of life so that they may acquire wisdom, understanding, discernment, a disciplined and prudent life, a commitment to doing what is right and just and fair, among other biblical virtues (Prov. 1:1–7). Central to this endeavor is the recognition that God is the giver of all of these attributes.

The Word of God

The way children come to faith in God is through hearing the Word of God (Rom. 10:17). We should speak, sing, and pray the Scriptures continually at home. God's Word should always be in front of our children.

The Scriptures speak of methods to help remember God's Word. Numbers 15:38 directs Jewish people to place tassels on their garments to remember God's commands. Other ways can be found. I have fond memories of visiting my grandparents' home and seeing Scripture verses on the walls. We can come up with creative methods to keep the primary content of our instruction, God's Word, always before our children.

As our children apply God's Word to their lives, they will grow in godly character. We should emphasize the Ten Commandments. Yeshua summed up these standards in Matthew 22:37–39: "'Love the Lord your God with all your heart and with all your soul and with all your mind.' This is the first and greatest commandment. And the second is like it: 'Love your neighbor as yourself.'"

The Golden Rule

The Golden Rule—"treat other people as you would like them to treat you" (Luke 6:31)—should be continually emphasized in the home. Helping children consider how they would want to be treated will provide them with instruction on how they should treat their siblings, friends, neighbors, adults, indeed, everyone they encounter in life.

The Jewish sage, Hillel, when asked by a non-Jew to be taught the totality of Torah while standing on one foot, replied, "What you find hateful do not do unto your friend. This is the entire Torah; the rest is commentary. Go study it" (*b. Sab.* 31a). Hillel's response, the converse of the Golden Rule, helps us to see the broad application of the Golden Rule.

When we need to discipline our child because he has hurt another child, we can exhort him to walk according to the Golden Rule. We can ask questions such as, "Would you want someone to hit you?" After your child says, "No," tell your child, "Then don't hit your brother."

Many applications could be made as you question your child according to the Golden Rule: "Would you want someone to call you bad names?"; "Would you want someone to gossip about you and tell others bad things about you?"; "Would you want someone to grab your toy from you?"; "Would you want someone to spit at you?"; "If you were a teacher, would you want one of your students to disrespect you?"; "If you were preparing a meal for others, would you want one of them to say they didn't like the food?" The Golden Rule should be a continual point of emphasis in the home, especially as we seek to help children learn how to treat others.

God's "One Another" Commands

Likewise, God's "one another" commands should be utilized. There are about thirty such commands in the Scriptures. Examples are "be kind and compassionate to one another" (Eph. 4:32), "honor one another above yourselves" (Rom. 12:10), "live in harmony with one another" (Rom. 12:16), and "encourage one another and build each other up" (I Thess. 5:11). These are useful in training.

An important "one another" command to teach is "greet one another" (Rom. 16:16). We should teach children how to greet others with enthusiasm, eye contact, and a smile. Shyness is not a legitimate excuse. While we should not get in a battle with our child over greeting an adult, we should also not excuse our child by saying, "She's just shy." If your child does not return a greeting, simply tell the person that you are working on this with your child.

There is a store near our house that has a tight parking lot. Often this store is very busy and the checkout lines can get exceedingly long. The cumulative effect can be a hostile atmosphere. My wife has even seen arguments between customers over their place in the checkout line. Well, one day I showed my children how to counter poor attitudes with positive attitudes. In our vehicle, we started greeting people and waving at them. People smiled and waved back. Proverbs 15:30 says, "A cheerful glance brings joy to the heart." Through a simple and sincere greeting, children can learn to spread the light of Yeshua to others.

Gratitude Instead of Griping

A major principle to be instilled is gratitude. Philippians 2:14–15 says, "Do everything without *kvetching* [complaining] or arguing, so that you may be blameless and pure children of God, without defect in the midst of a twisted and perverted generation, among whom you shine like stars in the sky." We need to train our children to avoid the tendency to complain and argue, and be thankful instead. How do we do this?

1 Thessalonians 5:18 says, "Give thanks in all circumstances." Giving heartfelt thanks to God and others is fundamental. Twerski

and Schwartz point out the positive effect that gratitude can have on children's character:

> The psychological consequences of gratitude can be far reaching. Gratitude is a positive effect; hence, it cannot co-exist with a negative effect, anymore than light can co-exist with darkness. If gratitude can be adequately developed, it can be the single most effective method for eliminating distress of various kinds. (Twerski and Schwartz, 211)

If our children catch the principle of walking with an attitude of gratitude, it will fundamentally change their character and their outlook on life.

Yeshua's Beatitudes, found in Matthew 5:1–12, are excellent for equipping children for life. I often tell my kids that "attitude is everything." For example, Matthew 5:5 says, "How blessed are the meek, for they will inherit the Land!" Attitudes such as meekness, which is strength under control, need to be encouraged.

Attitudes make such a difference in spreading Messiah's light to others. The Beatitudes proclaim how we are blessed, and our children need to live knowing that they are blessed. These statements of blessing apply to seemingly negative situations, such as being poor in spirit, mourning, having to show mercy to those who have injured us, having to make peace with others, being persecuted, being insulted, and being falsely accused. If our children can learn that they are still fundamentally blessed in these situations, they will have learned a very valuable lesson.

The Fruit of the Spirit

The fruit of the Spirit should also be emphasized. Galatians 5:22–23 explains: "The fruit of the Spirit is love, joy, peace, patience, kindness, goodness, faithfulness, humility, self control." The values listed in this passage imply the need to show empathy toward others.

Children naturally tend to look out more for themselves than for others. Showing concern for a fellow student, or a neighborhood friend who is not popular, is a worthy practice to instill.

The challenge is to help our children think of others first, before they think of themselves.

Yeshua's Character

Yeshua's character should be part of the content of instruction as well. Ephesians 5:1–2 says, "So imitate God, as his dear children; and live a life of love, just as also the Messiah loved us." Yeshua is humble (Phil. 2:5-8), merciful (Isa. 53), and loving (John 15:12-14). He is also committed (Matt. 16:24-25), courageous (Matt. 26:50-56), diligent (Luke 18:1-8), and decisive (Matt. 22:15-22).

The Scriptures tell us about many of Yeshua's character traits. Our Messiah is full of grace and truth (John 1:14), and we are called to speak the truth in love (Eph. 4:15). He is full of purpose (Luke 9:51). Yeshua is a suffering servant (Isa. 53), and he is holy (1 Pet. 1:15–16). Should our children seek to imitate our Lord? Absolutely! Our life in God is a continual process of our character becoming more and more like him.

Obedience, Honor, and Success

The virtues of obedience, honor, and success should be instilled in children. Ephesians 6:1–3 emphasizes the rightness of children obeying their parents. It also stresses the importance of honoring one's father and mother, and the blessing that follows: "that it may go well with you and that you may enjoy long life on the earth." Our children need to know that they will experience a meaningful and fulfilled life when they walk in the ways of the Lord.

Obedience to authorities God has placed in our lives is an essential lesson we must teach. Obedience is a prompt and willing submission to the authority's instructions. First-time obedience is an objective matter. Children either obey the first time or they do not. We should not allow them to delay compliance or only obey after nagging or after harshness of voice. One of my regular prayers is that my children will obey their parents, teachers, and coaches.

The people of Israel, who wandered in the desert forty years because of disobedience, had to learn to obey God before taking the Promised Land. In Joshua 1:7, God said, "Only be strong and very bold in taking care to follow all the Torah which Moshe my servant ordered you to follow; do not turn from it either to the right or to the left; then you will succeed wherever you go." Spiritually speaking, obedience is the straightest line between two points. If we desire our children to grow in character and in their walk with God, we will emphasize obedience.

As a school principal, I have seen that this area of instruction–to obey one's authorities–must be cultivated by the time children reach kindergarten. Children who have been trained to obey will learn better. They will know how to listen to their teachers' instructions; being a good listener is a prerequisite for being a good student. As Proverbs 18:13 says, "He who answers before listening–that is his folly and his shame."

When I was coaching Anna's basketball team of first and second graders, I taught the players how to play defense. I coached them to turn their heads back and forth to keep track of the ball in another player's possession, while at the same time sticking to the girl they were covering. At first, Anna thought she couldn't do it, but she sought to obey. Well, during a game, Silvia and I were overjoyed to see our daughter putting this defensive strategy into practice. Anna really listened!

Children will learn their lessons more quickly when they listen to their teachers. Rabbi Judith and Dr. Steven Abrams emphasize this point in their book *Jewish Parenting*:

> A good student . . . listens well, does not interrupt, thinks before offering an answer, does not wander off the topic, answers from a base of knowledge that is generally accepted, thinks in an orderly fashion, and knows the limits of his knowledge. A poor student, by implication, would not listen well, would interrupt, would answer questions impulsively, would not stay on task, would answer questions nonsensically, would exhibit disorganized thinking, and would

not be able to recognize the limits of his own knowledge. (Abrams and Abrams, 186)

The ability of children to listen and obey their parents and teachers is one determinant of their future success, especially in school.

Respect for Older People

Leviticus 19:32 says, "Stand up in the presence of a person with gray hair, show respect for the old; you are to fear your God; I am ADONAI." This verse suggests that honoring older people is an act of reverence toward God himself.

The content of instruction for our children should include ways to respect older people. We can teach our children to stand in the presence of older people; to use titles such as sir, ma'am, Mr., Mrs., and Ms. with the person's last name, not their familiar first name; and to greet them with a smile, eye contact, and a warm greeting: "Hello, Mr. Greenberg," or, "Good morning, Mr. Jones." While waiting for a table at a restaurant, our children can learn to honor older people by offering their seats to them and standing instead. As our children learn to humbly honor their elders, they will be laying the groundwork for a lifetime of success and favor with others.

Distinction Between Needs and Wants

Philippians 4:19 states, "My God will fill every need of yours according to his glorious wealth." Our Father promises to meet all of his children's needs, not necessarily their wants. We have a responsibility to meet our children's needs; however, to meet all of their wants would cause their character to be deficient.

Our children should be taught the difference between needs and wants. They want many things, including candy at the check-out line. My wife and I are endeavoring to teach our kids not to beg for things they want, but to allow their parents to surprise them with occasional treats. We teach them to make proper requests for needs.

Opportunities for Growth

Young people need to be given opportunities for growth, occasions when they can practice obedience. Character formation takes place in the context of relationships. With the proper guidance, children can learn teamwork and interpersonal skills while playing on athletic teams and participating in other group activities.

Children should be given regular tasks to reinforce the ethic of hard work and responsibility. As they get older, they should take on jobs, such as paper routes, which require them to answer to a person in authority. I am very grateful that my dad allowed my brothers and me to have paper routes at a young age. If we were late for the morning route because we slept in, or if we failed to deliver our papers, my dad did not cover for us. He made us deal with our managers ourselves. This provided us with training to develop a solid work ethic. We each had to take responsibility for accomplishing the job of delivering the papers in a timely manner. As youths, we gained a healthy respect for what it takes to earn money.

I believe that children should not receive monetary allowances for performing regular chores that are part of managing the household, such as making one's bed, cleaning one's room, helping with the dishes, taking out the trash, and vacuuming the living room. However, if they take on an extra task, a monetary value could be attached to it for its successful completion. Examples of these kinds of tasks might be planting flowers, washing the car, and helping with a home improvement project. Responsibilities and activities such as these are an essential part of the content of instruction because they help children grow godly character qualities through experience, while still under our parental guidance.

How to Make a Living

As children approach adulthood, they must learn how to "make a living." "The father must . . . teach his son a trade, for if he does not, it is likened to teaching him to be a thief, because he'll have to make money somehow. Therefore, the father is obligated to teach his son to make a living honestly" (Abrams and Abrams, 209). My father helped me to find productive work during my high school and college years. He didn't let me off the hook when it came to my need to make money to get through college. He also actively helped me to find a major that was a good fit.

Eventually, I did find my calling in teaching and discipling young people. However, I needed some fatherly guidance, as do most youth, to find my way. There will be times when our young people will need healthy doses of truth spoken into their lives. This will help them discover God's calling in their lives.

Chapter Nine

Setting Boundaries

OUR SOCIETY ESPOUSES a culture without boundaries. In the media, actors and directors are lauded for pushing the limits when it comes to violence, sexuality and speech. However, as believers, God calls us to walk within biblical boundaries. This ensures that we will walk in his protection and blessing.

Boundaries Established by God

God treats boundaries very seriously. Proverbs 23:10–11 says, "Don't move the ancient boundary stone or encroach on the land of the fatherless; for their Redeemer is strong; he will take up their fight against you." Even the waters of the earth have to stay within God's boundaries (Ps. 104:5–9). The boundaries that God has set in place are to be treated with utmost respect.

Boundaries have existed since the beginning of time. In the Garden of Eden, Adam and Eve were told, "You may freely eat from every tree in the garden except the tree of the knowledge of good and evil. You are not to eat from it, because on the day that you eat from it, it will become certain that you will die" (Gen. 2:16–17). Adam and Eve had boundaries within which they were free to work and eat. As long as they walked within those boundaries, they were blessed by the goodness of the garden. Psalm 16:6 says, "The boundary lines have fallen for me in pleasant places." That same psalm talks about walking in the Lord's security, on his path, and in his presence. The Lord's boundaries are not meant to make life miserable. We find freedom within boundaries.

The Need for Boundaries

Children need boundaries and find security within limits. They learn that it is bad for them to wander onto a street with oncoming cars. They learn to respect the wisdom of not crossing at a certain point. Proverbs 29:15 says, "The rod and rebuke give wisdom, but a child left to himself [a child without boundaries] brings shame on his mother."

My family lives in a townhouse within a court. Because vehicles drive through the neighborhood, we have had to set boundaries for our children when they play. For instance, up to a certain age they are not allowed to leave the court to play elsewhere without our permission. When our son Nehemiah was a toddler, we had to tell him to "stay in the yellow," an area in front of our home that had very little traffic. Nehemiah had to learn to stay within this boundary for his safety. Even though his siblings advanced so they could go further out, he had to stay within that boundary for his well being.

One boundary is time. Helping children make wise use of their time is important training. Ephesians 5:15–16 says, "Therefore, pay careful attention to how you conduct your life—live wisely, not unwisely. Use your time well, for these are evil days." We should help kids have an appropriate morning routine, including a daily quiet time of Scripture reading and prayer. We should establish an appropriate afternoon and evening schedule, including the accomplishment of daily chores and homework.

We should establish sleep patterns early in life. When infants and toddlers have set bedtimes and naptimes, they are more secure. Adequate rest also helps them be more pleasant. We should avoid allowing them to sleep in our bed. As a principal I have become aware that when this boundary is crossed, it is harmful to both the children and the husband and wife. Children wake up tired, and parents end up losing sleep and any semblance of romance as well.

Dealing With Homework

Regarding homework, it is important that we help children develop good study habits. We should establish a daily study time at an appropriate study station. Depending upon their maturity level, we will need to monitor this. Of course, needed boundaries should be established; the television, toys, and other gadgets should be off-limits during this period. We should establish clear boundaries for the content and the length of time for our children's television viewing, as well. As they learn to walk in the freedom of boundaries, children will understand that when it is time to play, they can play; when it is time to study, they are to study.

Children should learn to chip away at long-term assignments and regularly review academic material, a habit that will prepare them for upcoming assessments. As they avoid the trap of procrastination and instead learn to discipline their time, they will be prepared for the academic rigors of high school and college.

When we communicate and hold to consistent boundaries, we provide our children with a place of safety. As Proverbs 14:26–27 says, "In the fear of ADONAI is powerful security; for his children there will be a place of refuge. The fear of ADONAI is a fountain of life enabling one to avoid deadly traps." Although our young people may test our boundaries from time to time, they will learn to trust us. They ultimately find a place of refuge as they learn to walk within the wisdom of God's boundaries.

Our children need to know that we have moral convictions. They will ultimately appreciate and respect us for the loving stand we take. If we are consistent with boundaries based on God's Word, they will also learn to trust the Lord.

Accountability

In order for boundaries to be respected, we must provide account-ability. Children need to be held accountable for the standards that we set. For whatever boundary we have set, we must consistently correct our children when it is crossed.

Sin is missing the mark, like an arrow missing the bull's eye of the target. When we step outside the boundaries God has set for us, we miss the mark. Psalm 19:12–13 shares different levels (like ever-larger concentric circles around the bull's eye on an archer's target) of missing the boundaries for our lives:

> Who can discern unintentional sins?
> Cleanse me from hidden faults.
> Also keep your servant from presumptuous sins,
> so that they won't control me.
> Then I will be blameless
> and free of great offense.

Unintentional Sins

We all commit unintentional sins in our lives. That is why it is important to allow spouses and parents to correct us. As we allow an editor to help us find grammatical and spelling errors in a written work, we should allow the influential people in our lives to help us recognize our mistakes. Parents should point out their children's unintentional sins so that they can grow in godliness.

Hidden Faults

Hidden faults are like blind spots when driving a car. It is up to parents to help their children see character weaknesses so that they can be addressed. People usually like to keep hidden faults exactly that way–hidden. This is especially true for children. If they choose to continue in these errors, then we should no longer classify them as "hidden faults," but as "presumptuous sins."

Presumptuous Sins

Often it is difficult to distinguish between a hidden fault or a presumptuous sin. Children must be held accountable for committing presumptuous sins, those they know to be wrong. If they actively give themselves to purposeful sin, then that sin will become their master. It will control them. If we allow them to live a life of sin, they will be in danger of bigger sins.

1 Corinthians 5:6–7 says, "Don't you know the saying, 'It takes only a little *hametz* [leaven] to leaven a whole batch of dough?' Get rid of the old *hametz*, so that you can be a new batch of dough." Children must be held accountable for the "little" sins. If we allow a "little" sin, then that sin will get larger and larger. After awhile, sin will be their master. Instead, if we are diligent to correct the "little" sins in love and faithfulness, we will help our children walk within godly boundaries.

When they become settled and at peace within these boundaries, it enables us to teach them. We can let them know that there are many blessings for those who walk in God's path, including abundant life, direction, freedom, security, and wisdom for living (Ps. 119:35, 105, 110, 165).

Chapter Ten

Training Techniques

"TRAIN A CHILD in the way he should go, and when he is old he will not turn from it" (Prov. 22:6) is a Scripture that is often spoken by believing parents as a self-encouragement that eventually their child will return to God's ways. However, in order for this verse to mean what God intended, actual training must occur. Webster's Dictionary provides the following definition for the word "train": "To exercise; to discipline; to teach and form by practice."

When our daughter was three years old, my wife had an interesting conversation with her. After we had put Anna to bed, she began crying. Silvia went in and held her for a while. She then asked, "Mommy, are you going to buy me flowers when I get married?"

"Of course, we'll buy you the most beautiful flowers in the world," her mom responded.

"Then what do I do?"

"You'll walk down the aisle and marry your husband," her mom said.

"And then can I have children?"

My wife, of course, replied, "Yes."

Anna was very excited to find that out.

Silvia continued, "But first, you have to go to school, high school, college, work a little, and then you get married."

Anna agreed and asked, "But who will I marry? I want to marry Daddy. I want him to be my husband." My wife proceeded to explain that Daddy was Mommy's husband but that God would show Anna whom to marry when the time came.

Children will ask questions about life. When the opportunities arise, we need to be ready to steer them in the right direction. Training occurs during times of conflict and non-conflict. Look for these opportunities.

We should not wait for our preschool children to decide which path they want to follow. Instead, we should place our children on God's path, the path leading to life. In other words, we should direct our children to take the narrow path. Training of children is a daily, active, ongoing task to which we will be dedicated until our children practice God's standards with consistency.

Ephesians 6:4 says, "Fathers, do not exasperate your children; instead, bring them up in the training and instruction of the LORD." Look closely at the sequence of that verse. Raising children involves both training and instruction. Proper training is required for true instruction to occur.

Proverbs 29:15 warns parents that "a child left to himself brings shame on his mother." Eli suffered the consequences of not controlling his sons: "For I told him that I would judge his family forever because of the sin he knew about; his sons made themselves contemptible, and he failed to restrain them" (1 Sam. 3:13). Parents must first be able to control their children through training before they can instruct them.

Eli was judged because he failed to restrain his sons. We will be judged if we fail to restrain our children. This includes physically restraining them, especially for younger children. When my daughter was two years old, my wife and I were very embarrassed while eating at a restaurant with our extended family. Anna threw a temper tantrum and we had a terrible time with her. We realized that we had to physically control her by embracing her and not allow her to have emotional outbursts. Obviously, we should never physically abuse our children; however, we will need to exercise legitimate physical restraint to require our children to learn to resist their sinful nature and to comply with our instructions.

Once we have proper control of our children through training, we are then able to instruct them. God calls us to teach our children the right way. This instruction goes counter to many modern parenting philosophies, which tell parents to allow children–even young children–to find their own way. On the contrary, we should not shy away from actively influencing our children in God's ways. Three techniques that God provides are repetition, imagery, and drawing out understanding.

Repetition

A key method of training is repetition: "Teach [God's words] carefully to your children, talking about them when you sit at home, when you are traveling on the road, when you lie down and when you get up" (Deut. 11:19). As the passage indicates, we should use every opportunity we have to teach God's Word to our children. This should include memorization of Scripture passages. Children's minds become sharp through regular meditation on the Word of God. Furthermore, their character will be strengthened: "I treasure your word in my heart, so that I won't sin against you" (Ps. 119:11).

Memorizing verses such as 1 Corinthians 10:13 provides our children with strength in times of temptation: "No temptation has seized you except what is common to man. And God is faithful; he will not let you be tempted beyond what you can bear. But when you are tempted, he will also provide a way out so that you can stand up under it." Scripture memorization and meditation will strengthen our children's minds and hearts.

Imagery

God's Word advocates the use of images and signs to train our children. He knew about visual, auditory, and kinesthetic learners before any of us! He made exhaustive use of imagery in order to teach the children of Israel. Note what he told Joshua:

> When the whole nation had finished crossing the Jordan, the LORD said to Joshua, "Choose twelve men from among

the people, one from each tribe, and tell them to take up
twelve stones from the middle of the Jordan from right
where the priests stood and to carry them over with you
and put them down at the place where you stay tonight."
So Joshua called together the twelve men he had appointed
from the Israelites, one from each tribe, and said to them,
"Go over before the ark of the LORD your God into the
middle of the Jordan. Each of you is to take up a stone on
his shoulder, according to the number of the tribes of the
Israelites, to serve as a sign among you. *In the future, when
your children ask you, 'What do these stones mean?' tell them
that the flow of the Jordan was cut off before the ark of the
covenant of the LORD. When it crossed the Jordan, the waters of
the Jordan were cut off. These stones are to be a memorial to the
people of Israel forever."* (Josh. 4:1–7, italics added)

God knew that when the Israelites saw the memorial, they would
ask questions. Something was different and the children would
want to know why. Thus, God was able to ensure that the Israelites
would know their nation's history. Imagery can be used with children, too. Just be creative and you will come up with ideas.

Drawing Out Understanding

God wants us to "draw out" understanding from the hearts of our
children. In education circles, theorists and practitioners debate
whether the learner should be treated as a cup which the teacher
is simply filling up with facts or whether the learner should be
viewed as a muscle that is exercised for greater and greater effectiveness. Both perspectives are required in training children.

Proverbs 20:5 is applicable to our parenting call: "The purposes
of a man's heart are deep waters, but a man of understanding
draws them out." In some cases, we are to train our children in
the exact way to do things; in other cases, we need to draw out
our children as we guide the conversation and help them process
issues. As a teenager and a young man, I would often go out for
breakfast with my father. He would spend time with me in order

to "draw out" the deep purposes of my heart: my struggles, my doubts, my desires, and ultimately my purpose in life.

There are no "quick fixes" for training our children in the Lord; discipleship takes years and years. However, the earlier we begin to hold our children accountable to God's standards and walk with them down that path, the easier and more successful our task will be. Remember, training in most things is a daily activity. The job of raising children is hard work, but it is worth it!

Chapter Eleven

Training Steps

IN HIS BOOK *WHAT THE BIBLE SAYS ABOUT . . . Child Training*, J. Richard Fugate advocates four steps that parents should take to train their children: setting standards, rebuking, forgiving after confession, and punishment (204–205). I have personally found that consistent and proper implementation of these steps is necessary in order for them to have their desired effect.

Setting Standards

Romans 4:15 says, "Where there is no law, there is also no violation." We cannot expect children to know what to do if we do not tell them what to do. They cannot be held accountable for a misdeed, and indeed have not transgressed, if they have not been told that such a thing is a transgression. We must first set the standard with our children. God calls us to set standards that agree with the Scriptures.

In some cases, we should warn of the penalty for breaking the standard. Children should be able to state the standard and the penalty in their own words. That way we can be confident that they have heard and understood.

Rebuking

The second step in training your child is to rebuke him when the standard is broken. Ephesians 5:13–14 expresses the purpose of the rebuke: "But everything exposed by the light becomes visible, for it is light that makes everything visible." A rebuke is designed to bring the wrongdoing into the light. The rebuke calls sin what it is—sin.

The rebuke needs to be stated so that your child understands what he has done wrong. Sometimes he will try to deceive himself into thinking that what he did was not actually wrong. You must establish in his mind and heart that he is guilty of wrongdoing.

Ask your child, "What did you do?" to give him the opportunity to confess. For young children, you should avoid asking your child, "Why did you do that?" You should avoid looking for excuses for your child's wrongdoing (Fugate, 264). Exodus 32:21–24 tells of how Moses asked Aaron for an explanation of his actions, and Aaron tried to transfer the guilt of his sin to others. To avoid conflict or to avoid punishing a child, parents often try to justify their child's wrongdoing. God calls us to be different. We should take the long view with our children and not justify their actions when they miss the mark. We need to use each opportunity we are given to train them in godliness. They must learn to take personal responsibility for their actions without shifting the blame to others. Rather, they should be trained to confess their wrongdoing, which leads us to step three.

Forgiving After Confession

Once your child has taken responsibility for his sin by acknowledging his wrong action as well as his guilt, you should quickly forgive him. Leviticus 26:40 speaks of the Israelites' confession of sins, and then Leviticus 26:41 describes the payment for sin. These verses illustrate the principle that confession of sin comes before the penalty. Fugate comments on the nature of confession:

> If a child will agree with his parents when they declare him wrong, he will not need the physical pressure of chastisement

to face his guilt. All he needs to say is, "Yes, I was wrong," or, "It was my fault." Whether a child is totally repentant internally is not the parents' responsibility to determine. They should accept any admission of guilt that is given with a proper attitude. (Fugate, 273)

Once your child confesses his wrong, you should unconditionally forgive him. With confession, his heart will become tender and prepared for a penalty.

Punishment

The punishment is usually administered after confession and forgiveness. This is how God deals with us. Numbers 14:17–23 tells of God's forgiveness of his people's rebellion, yet still punishing them for their disobedience. Psalm 99:8 declares, "You were to Israel a forgiving God, though you punished their misdeeds." After confessing his guilt, King David had to pay the penalty for his sin of killing Uriah and taking his wife Bathsheba (2 Sam. 12:9–22; 13:28; 18:14–15).

Your administration of punishment should be objective. It should be a simple matter of restitution. The penalty should match the offense. If your child uses his crayons to draw on the kitchen wall, you should have him clean (or help clean) the mess and then not allow him to use his crayons for an appropriate length of time. You can be creative with your matching penalties. I personally prefer giving my children push-ups. Depending on the offense, I give them anywhere from five to twenty-five push-ups. (In the process, they also develop some upper body strength.)

We can use many different types of matching penalties. If our children don't come home on time from a neighbor's house, then they forgo the privilege of visiting their neighbor's house for a week. If they keep their bedroom a mess, perhaps extra vacuuming is appropriate. If they carelessly damage another's property, they can do extra chores to earn the money for the property's restoration. Regarding physical abuse of others, the penalty is receiving pain, or chastisement, which will be discussed more fully in a later chapter. Children learn through receiving a matching penalty because the penalty itself reinforces that their specific behavior was wrong.

Finally, you should administer the punishment without partiality: "You are not to show favoritism when judging, but give equal attention to the small and to the great. No matter how a person presents himself, don't be afraid of him; because the decision is God's" (Deut. 1:17).

After you set the standard with your child and determine to hold him accountable for obedience, you must follow through. When he comes to the realization that he cannot get his own way, he will find security within your loving and consistent discipline.

Resisting the Urge to Be Lenient

When administering punishment, we must resist the urge to be lenient in the name of "giving grace." It is best for children's character that they pay the price for their wrongdoing. Being consistent with a matching penalty helps them understand that there is a penalty for sin. As they grow older, they will take seriously the fact that Messiah paid the ultimate penalty for our sin. "For the wages of sin is death, but the gift of God is eternal life in Messiah Yeshua our LORD" (Rom. 6:23).

We should avoid training wrong habits into children. Often parents teach their children that they do not have to obey the first time instructions are given, or even worse—they only have to obey after they are threatened. To avoid conflict, parents may allow their child to give excuses for their behavior and release them from responsibility for wrongdoing.

To illustrate this process of holding children responsible for their actions, our family has set the standard in the area of lying. Our children know that it is wrong for them to lie to us. If our son were to lie to us about cleaning his room, we would rebuke him for the lie. We would bring the sin into the light and be sure that our son knew that he had done wrong. Next we would have our son say, "I was wrong for lying. Will you forgive me?" After forgiving our son, we would then decide on an appropriate matching penalty. Finally, we would finish the discipline with a hug and a reassurance of our love for him.

God calls us to set clear standards for our children, to rebuke them in order to bring sin into the light, to forgive them after they confess their wrongdoing, and to provide a just matching penalty for their offense. If we consistently follow this order for disciplining, we can be confident that we are training them according to God's Word. If we courageously and consistently apply positive boundaries, we will reap the reward of a healthy relationship with our children, one that will extend into their adult years.

Chapter Twelve

Dealing With Rebellion

JOSHUA 22:16 STATES, "What is this treachery that you have committed against the God of Isra'el, turning away today from following ADONAI, in that you have built yourselves an altar, thus rebelling today against ADONAI?" As this passage indicates, rebellion is an act of turning against authority instituted by God. Indeed, when our children openly resist our authority, they are in rebellion. Rebellion concerns the will of the child. Will the child submit to the parent willingly, or will he exert his own will above that of the parent?

Rebellion can be expressed overtly and covertly. Children may refuse to listen to their parents' instructions. They may express rebellion through temper tantrums and by stubbornly refusing to obey. They may walk away in defiance of our authority. Children also may not accept correction by stubbornly arguing that what occurred was not their fault. We should never tolerate these overt expressions.

Anna was born with a very strong will. Even at a young age, she exerted her will in a rebellious manner and threw some serious temper tantrums. Silvia and I knew that we needed to work hard to win the battles with her. This meant that we had to restrain her temper tantrums. For a season, we were aware that it was a critical time to establish our parental control for her sake. This was a process that required consistency and hard work. Today, Anna, still strong-willed, has learned to control her will and to obey her parents.

Passive Rebellion

Children will sometimes express passive rebellion. Although expressed differently, passive rebellion is just as serious as overt rebellion. The child may comply externally; however, internal resentment has built up within the child. In 1 Samuel 15, when Saul did not completely obey the Lord's instructions, Samuel rebuked him. Saul went on to explain how he did obey the Lord, justifying his actions. However, Samuel answered him with the following:

> Does ADONAI take as much pleasure in burnt offerings and sacrifices as in obeying what ADONAI says? Surely obeying is better than sacrifice, and heeding orders than the fat of rams. For rebellion is like the sin of sorcery, stubbornness like the crime of idolatry. Because you have rejected the word of ADONAI, he too has rejected you as king. (1 Sam. 15:22–23)

Passive rebellion is expressed when a child partially obeys on his own terms. He may do the task required in a different way than what was instructed by the parents. He may appear to be compliant, listening quietly to his parents' instructions, but inside he knows he is going to do things his own way. The child appears to have a level of obedience; however, underneath, the child is choosing not to fully obey. Passive rebellion starts with a "hidden mental attitude" and eventually comes out into the open through "facial expressions of disrespect, disgust, or anger" (Fugate, 144).

My son, Caleb, who is naturally a very compliant boy, has struggled with a complaining attitude. Although his attitude was not expressed as overt rebellion, Silvia and I had to sit down with him and share that we were going to hold him accountable for his attitude.

All children have their issues. With some children, the issues are obvious; with others, the issues are more hidden. Parents should not think that one child is "perfect" while their other child "has his issues." It is important to address more passive forms of disobedience, even if our children seem to be very compliant.

Some children will not argue or throw a temper tantrum. Instead, they will make a sad face or walk away looking hurt. This kind of passive rebellion needs to be addressed forthrightly. It is critical that we bring any areas of disobedience into the light and hold our children accountable for them, even if we think we can tolerate this behavior. No matter what form it takes, rebellion is rebellion. We cannot expect rebellion to just go away. Rebellion must be addressed and corrected, and the earlier the better.

Sometimes parents do not want to confront their children's rebellion head on. They may fear that their children will rebel further. They may not want to face the conflict. Therefore, many parents use threats: "If you don't clean your room, I won't buy you that doll you want." Parents will bribe their children to do what they want them to do: "If you behave while we're at the store, I'll give you a candy bar at the end." They might try to distract their child's attention from wrongdoing. This is the wrong approach.

In addition, we should not reason with our young children. While we should provide our young child with easy-to-understand biblical principles, we should not spend a lot of time explaining the many reasons we want them to do something. Also, when we give younger children a command and they ask, "Why?" with an obstinate attitude, we should not get distracted from requiring their obedience.

Chastisement Used for Rebellion

Ultimately, the only way to control rebellion is to use chastisement. "Chastisement . . . refers to the use of a rod to inflict pain sufficient to correct a child's rebellion or to restrain a child from willful disobedience" (Fugate, 291). Proverbs 13:24 states: "He who spares the rod hates his son, but he who loves him is careful to discipline him." When a child is in rebellion, he is out from under his parents' protective covering. Chastising the child, when he is in this unsafe position, is a loving act.

Other Scriptures express the need for chastisement:

> Folly is bound up in the heart of a child, but the rod of discipline will drive it far from him. (Prov. 22:15)
>
> Do not withhold discipline from a child; if you punish him with the rod, he will not die. Punish him with the rod and save his soul from death. (Prov. 23:13–14)
>
> The rod of correction imparts wisdom, but a child left to himself disgraces his mother. (Prov. 29:15)
>
> Those whom I love I rebuke and discipline. So be earnest, and repent. (Rev. 3:19)

We should never slap our children, shove them, or physically abuse them in any way. Rather, we should use a rod, a neutral object, never our hands.

Chastisement should mainly be used when children defy authority. We must use judgment regarding the number of strokes needed and not hurt our children. Before chastising our children, we must not be angry. We must be self-controlled and have a calm attitude. Chastisement requires wisdom and restraint. We should not use the rod for "punishment" unless our child physically and purposefully hurt someone else.

Distinction Between Chastisement and Punishment

Chastisement is used to control a child's rebellion, the willful rejection of authority. On the other hand, punishment is used to administer justice, to set a penalty that matches the breaking of a standard. Leviticus 24:17–22 expresses the principle that when there is a transgression, fair restitution should involve a matching penalty.

We need to use our common sense to establish appropriate penalties. Use of the rod will not be appropriate for most offenses. Chastisement should only be used as a legitimate physical force to bring a rebellious child into submission.

We parents need to be willing to use the rod. The rod is a biblically sanctioned instrument to bring a rebellious child under control. We should not use our hands, our belt, or any other object for rebellion. When our children rebel, we should lovingly and courageously apply the rod for the sake of our children's character.

Fruit of Chastisement

Hebrews 12:11 says, "Now, all discipline, while it is happening, does indeed seem painful, not enjoyable; but for those who have been trained by it, it later produces its peaceful fruit, which is righteousness." Often parents, specifically mothers, will shy away from the discipline of chastisement. They do not want to see their child experience short-term pain. However, God calls us to look out for the long-term good of our children. As our children receive this consistent training, they will be steered in the direction of righteousness and peace. Ultimately, they will be grateful to us for the love that we expressed to them through our faithful discipline.

Once when we were having friends over for dinner, I had to chastise my daughter. One person, who didn't have children at the time, was surprised that after I chastised my daughter, she returned to the table very happy as if "nothing had happened." "It works," he commented. Indeed, God's method for dealing with rebellion does work. It helps children shun the misery of poor attitudes and instead walk in peace, joy, and righteousness.

Chapter Thirteen

Relational Communication

I T IS CRITICAL THAT WE COMMUNICATE in ways pleasing to the Lord as we train our children. I often say to my children when they are tempted to be worried or afraid, "Think about Jesus!" One Mother's Day, while Silvia was still in bed, our two oldest children came into the bedroom and gave my wife hand-made gifts for her special day. When our three-year-old son Nehemiah saw what was happening, he did not want to be left out of the joy of giving to his mommy, so he went to his bedroom and got a number of gifts; in fact, he returned with quite a few of his precious toys which Silvia graciously accepted. Hoping that Nehemiah would take his toys back to his bedroom, she told him that all the toys were crowding between the side of the bed and the nearby wall and she might get hurt trying to get past all of her new gifts. Nehemiah had the perfect response for my wife's concerns. He said, "Just think about Jesus!" Silvia and I were overcome with joy: Nehemiah had listened to his daddy's voice! Our communication was getting through to his heart and mind.

Caring Communication

Our challenge is to communicate in ways that get through to our children's hearts and minds, whether they are three or fifteen years old. I am grateful for how my parents practiced communication with my brothers and me in our youth. They patiently communicated in ways pleasing to the Lord, not reacting to us, or becoming flabbergasted by us. By doing so, they left open avenues for communication.

Sometimes it meant that my mother would simply communicate with God when one of us was going through a trial or was sitting on the fence on a moral issue. She would come into our bedroom at night, sit down or kneel by the bed, and pray. She expressed her care for us by interceding for us, many times without our knowledge, when she knew we were at critical junctures.

Other times, my father would come to our room and talk with us one-on-one when it was obvious we were dealing with a personal hurt or trial. Perhaps we demonstrated a closed spirit by not being talkative; he would patiently ask questions. If we were tight-lipped about it, he would persevere, not giving up, until we would start to open up our hearts and communicate. He would be careful not to react, or get defensive, when we would say something critical of him or my mom. Instead, he practiced excellent listening skills, drew us out, and helped us to come to a godly resolution. He wouldn't indulge our fleshly attitudes, but would righteously help us come to a God-honoring perspective.

Revelation 3:20 says, "Here, I'm standing at the door, knocking. If someone hears my voice and opens the door, I will come in to him and eat with him, and he will eat with me." We need to imitate Yeshua in this regard as we approach sensitive areas in our child's life. The image of God standing at the door and knocking, waiting patiently to be invited into a person's life, is a powerful picture. Many times we will need to patiently wait until our young person opens the door and invites us into his life.

After our child invites us in and we have listened to him, then we are able to provide instruction in biblical principles, particularly for teens. We will be able to share the reasons for the rules that they have learned, and the reasons for walking in godliness. We will be able to help them appreciate God's blessings.

Keeping Our Word

In building this trusting relationship, our children must know that our word means something; keeping our word builds trust. An anecdote about Silvia reinforces this principle. During a winter snowstorm, my wife promised our children that she would go sledding with them. Silvia is not overly enthusiastic about snow activities, and would have been very happy if our children had forgotten about what she had said. Yet, she realized that she needed to follow through on her promise and got out in the snow with the rest of us (and she enjoyed sledding down the big hill).

Over the years, I have been keenly aware that when I tell my children I will do something, it is imperative that I keep my word. If my communication is to mean anything to them, I must have their trust so they can depend on what I say. Telushkin emphasizes this point:

> If a parent promises a gift to a child and doesn't bring it, or agrees to take a child on a trip and then cancels, the child's initial response will be disappointment . . . . if such unfulfilled promises occur often enough, he or she will eventually conclude that that is how the real world works, that even when you assure someone you are going to do something for them, there is no need to follow through on your word. (Telushkin, 415)

Communicating Nurture

There are three ways to communicate a nurturing relationship to our children each day. First, "physical touch." Each of our children should feel care by being hugged daily. We can never share too many hugs or kisses. Whether it's my ten-year-old daughter wanting to dance with me in the kitchen or my four-year-old son wanting to wrestle with me in the living room, I always try to provide my children with a lot of positive physical contact. Second, our children should receive "focused attention" daily. Instead of giving partial attention while watching television, we need to stop what we are doing, listen to our child, and give our full attention. Third, we need to establish "eye contact" with our children when talking together. We should look each child in the eye to communicate our love daily. Making huge deposits of love and favor toward our children by looking deep into their eyes is a special joy that should be cherished. Communicating love in these ways will help fill our child's emotional love bank (Switzer and Switzer, "Secrets in the Adventure of Family Life," session five).

Covenantal Communication

My parents, brothers, and I had periodic family talks at the dinner table or even at a retreat center. We would come together to spend time as a family or to talk about a family issue. My parents had excellent listening skills and patiently asked questions to get to the heart of things. This skill is especially important when our child's spirit seems closed and is manifesting anger or a stubborn refusal to enter into the life of the family.

Our challenge is to stay with the process until we are able to draw out what is in our children's hearts. Often it is a matter of giving the necessary time to our children. When we persevere in this way, we demonstrate our covenant love to our children.

Edifying Speech

We need to set a high standard of communication. Ephesians 4:29 says: "Let no harmful language come from your mouth, only good words that are helpful in meeting the need, words that will benefit those who hear them." Communication in the home needs to be encouraging. Of course, parents are the first examples of this in their relationship as husband and wife. Yes, arguments occur between parents; however, when they occur and our children hear us, we need to come back to our children and let them know that we have worked things out. We also need to apologize for upsetting the peace of the home. We need to be examples of positive communication and hold our children accountable for their communication with one another as well.

The Influence of Grandparents

Within godly boundaries, grandparents can be important influences in the lives of our children. Proverbs 17:6 says, "Grandchildren are the crown of the aged, while the glory of children is their ancestors." As we all know, there is a special relationship between grandparents and grandchildren. Sometimes we say that grandparents get to "spoil" their grandchildren; however, I believe that God has a great purpose for grandparents.

Deuteronomy 4:9 provides instruction for grandparents: "Only be careful, and watch yourselves diligently as long as you live, so that you won't forget what you saw with your own eyes, so that these things won't vanish from your hearts. Rather, *make them known to your children and grandchildren*" (italics added). God calls grandparents to "finish strong" and to remember the awesome deeds God has done. This is their testimony in the Lord! As they do so, they will be able to share with their grandchildren what they have seen over the years in their walk with the Lord. Their testimony of God's work in their life will be a powerful influence on your children. Even at the age of 87, my grandfather sat with my three brothers and me and shared with us principles from God's Word about family life, raising children, and living for the Lord.

For me personally, my grandparents have been a source of strength. Their years of living for the Lord, walking in Messiah-like character, and passing on a godly heritage have been a rich source of motivation in my life. Grandparents can and should be a powerful, positive influence in the lives of our children.

Communicating With God as a Family

Philippians 4:6–7 says, "Don't worry about anything; on the contrary, make your requests known to God by prayer and petition, with thanksgiving. Then God's *shalom*, passing all understanding, will keep your hearts and minds safe in union with the Messiah Yeshua." We need to be quick to go to God with requests when a need arises.

As our children grow up, they should find it normal to go to prayer immediately when there is a worry, a health concern, a need for provision, or another person's need. Ultimately, the goal is that our children develop a trust in God, knowing that he is in control, and that we can go to him at any time with our requests. Prayer should be a normal aspect of our home life.

We who are children of God have a defining characteristic: We can hear his voice! Of the shepherd, Yeshua said in John 10:4, "The sheep follow him because they recognize his voice." As sheep of the Good Shepherd, we can hear the voice of the Shepherd.

When we want our children to come home from being at the playground, we call, "OK guys; time to come in!" Our own children come home, but not the other children. Our children know and trust their own parents' voices. And when our children respond with prompt obedience, we feel great joy. Likewise, as our children grow in their relationship with God, they learn to recognize God's voice in the quietness of their hearts. They will discern the Lord's voice calling them to obedience and giving them encouragement as they grow.

My wife and I encourage our children to have a personal "quiet time" before breakfast. They read from the Scriptures or from an age-appropriate devotional book. We encourage them to communicate with God through prayer, and we help them to understand that an important part of prayer is listening to God's voice.

In our society there are many loud noises that clamor for attention. Our children can easily end up listening to those voices unless they learn to hear God's voice, the still, small voice of the Good Shepherd in the quietness of their hearts. Our children can learn to trust the leading of the *Ruach HaKodesh* (Holy Spirit), their Counselor, as they commit their way to him (Prov. 3:5–6). Whether it is daily choices or major life decisions, they can learn to seek God's voice for direction.

Chapter Fourteen

Using the *Sh'ma* as a Teaching Model

THE *SH'MA* (HEAR) in Deuteronomy 6:4–9 provides us with a strategy for teaching children. The passage begins with the words, "Hear, Isra'el! ADONAI our God, ADONAI is one... you are to love ADONAI your God with all your heart, all your being and all your resources" (Deut. 6:4–5). The basic instruction here is that all of our life is to be an expression of love toward the one true God, including following his decrees. Instruction of our children should ultimately find its end in a love for God.

The passage continues, "These commandments that I give you today are to be upon your hearts. Impress them on your children" (Deut. 6:6–7a). The implication of these words is that God's commands are to be upon our hearts. Our values need to be God's values, and we cannot expect God's commands to be impressed upon our children if we have not embraced them ourselves. Moreover, it is important to note that God has given this educational strategy to us, not to the government or to anyone else.

After telling the Israelites to "impress" his commands upon their children, God gives them the specific method for doing so:

> You are to talk about them when you sit at home, when
> you are traveling on the road, when you lie down and when
> you get up. Tie them on your hand as a sign, put them at
> the front of a headband around your forehead, and write
> them on the door-frames of your house and on your gates.
> (Deut. 6:7–9)

God's method for impressing his commands on children's hearts
and minds is for the parents to integrate his Word into their lives.
There should be a never-ending focus on making God and his ways
the center of children's lives, whether at work, rest, or play. The
Abrams advocate the use of the *Sh'ma* (Deut. 6:4) as a framework
for communicating values to our young people (245), particularly
in difficult situations. Deuteronomy 6:4 proclaims, "*Sh'ma, Yisra'el!*
ADONAI *Eloheinu,* ADONAI *echad* [Hear, Isra'el! ADONAI our God, ADO-
NAI is one]." They share how each of the six words of Deuteronomy
6:4 have significance for teaching children.

Sh'ma-Hear

We need to "hear" our children. They need to know that we care
by our listening.

This principle of listening, or hearing others, is important in
all of our relationships, especially with our children. James 1:9
tells us, "My dear brothers, take note of this: Everyone should *be
quick to listen*, slow to speak and slow to become angry" (italics
added). When our children want to talk with us, we need to give
them our full attention.

With one of my sons, I have had to work at not exasperating
him by interrupting him before he could get out all of his words.
Proverbs 29:20 says, "Do you see a man who speaks in haste?
There is more hope for a fool than for him." We need to be careful to allow our children to get all of their words out and give
them the satisfaction that they are able to communicate with us in
a way that we "hear" them.

As a principal, I often have to catch myself in this area. I want
to jump in there and give my two cents about a situation. Instead,

I have to discipline myself to let the other person share all of what he or she wants to say, whether it is simply an administrative matter or a personal concern.

Matthew 18:15–16 says, "If your brother sins against you, go and show him his fault, just between the two of you. *If he listens to you, you have won your brother over.* But if he will not listen, take one or two others along, so that 'every matter may be established by the testimony of two or three witnesses'" (italics added). Simply listening or hearing someone out is a very powerful act! It takes time and it is not always the most efficient activity, but we can save ourselves a lot of trouble simply by listening.

Matthew 11:28–29, which tells us how we can come to the Father to gain rest for our souls, can guide us in how to listen to our children: "Come to me, all of you who are struggling and burdened, and I will give you rest. Take my yoke upon you and learn from me, because I am gentle and humble in heart, and you will find rest for your souls." When our young people desire to communicate with us, may they find rest. When they are ready to talk, may we not be hurried. When they come to us, may we avoid rushing them, "Yes. Yes. What do you want?" Instead, we need to look our young people in the face, affirm them, and let them unhurriedly talk with us. May they find rest.

When my son Nehemiah was almost two years old, he touched me tremendously, bringing tears to my eyes on one occasion. After dinner one evening, we had had a time of wrestling, tickling, and praising Yeshua. Nehemiah had been playing hard and sweating. Well, it came time for me to tell his siblings to get ready for bed, and I was busy cleaning up the kitchen from dinner. Then he brought me a water bottle, requesting me to open it because he was thirsty. I was in a hurry to get everything done and I said, "No, Nehemiah," and I put the bottle in the refrigerator. A couple of minutes later, he brought me another water bottle, again requesting a drink. (We had water bottles lying around the kitchen because we had used them at his sister's soccer practice earlier that evening.) This time, I relented a little, saying in effect, "Not now, Nehemiah, we're going to brush your teeth soon; you'll get water then." Then, a few minutes later, he came to me, lugging Anna's soccer backpack and trying to pull out her soccer water bottle from the side pouch. At that moment, I just had to stop. I sat down, opened the water bottle, and let my son drink as much water as he wanted. I paused and let him quench his thirst. Nehemiah didn't throw any tantrums; he was simply persistent in his own appealing way. I was moved that a boy not quite two years old could teach his daddy a very valuable life lesson.

When we follow the *Sh'ma* and stop to hear our children, we communicate care to them by letting them voice their concerns, their problems, whatever is on their hearts or minds. We put our children at ease when we are willing to listen to them, enabling them to relax in our presence.

Yisra'el-Israel

After we have heard our children out, we can communicate the values of Israel, the values of the Word of God.

The second Hebrew word in the *Sh'ma* is *Yisra'el*. God says, "Hear, Isra'el!" One can see the word *Yisra'el* here as symbolic, not only of the nation of Israel, but also of everything that makes Israel a distinct nation, a separate people. *Yisra'el* includes Torah, and by extension for us as Messianic believers, the whole counsel of the Word of God.

So when our child comes to share with us, we need to be ready to take the time to hear and listen to him. As we are listening, we should consider what God's Word says about the matter at hand.

ADONAI

The name ADONAI points to the covenant-keeping nature of God (Exod. 3:15; 34:5–10). He is a compassionate and merciful father:

> Bless ADONAI, my soul,
> and forget none of his benefits!
> He forgives all your offenses,
> he heals all your diseases,
> he redeems your life from the pit,
> he surrounds you with grace and compassion,

> he contents you with good as long as you live,
> so that your youth is renewed like an eagle's. . . .
> adonai is merciful and compassionate,
> slow to anger and rich in grace. . . .
> Just as a father has compassion on his children,
> adonai has compassion on those who fear him.
> (Ps. 103:2–5, 8, 13)

We should be like ADONAI in the way we relate to our children.

Eloheinu-Our God

Eloheinu speaks of a God (*Elohim*) of might and justice:

> *Elohim* [God] stands in the divine assembly;
> there with the *elohim* [judges], he judges…
> Rise up, *Elohim*, and judge the earth,
> for all the nations are yours. (Ps. 82:1, 8)

Eloheinu points to the great Judge who presides over all the earth. His strength no one can resist; he will administer his truth and justice to the nations. Like *Eloheinu*, we should speak truth and justice into the lives of our children. At the same time, we do not want to react with harshness when they do wrong. In my experience as a principal, I have seen parents expect perfection from their children and react harshly to them when their children miss the mark. They end up actually training their children to lie to them out of fear of harsh retribution. For instance, parents might tell their child, "I don't want to see any discipline slips from you!" Our children take statements like that literally. They do not want to disappoint us and may be tempted to hide the teacher's disciplinary memos that are sent home.

It is important that we communicate the heart of ADONAI first to our children through unconditional love and acceptance. Then we can proceed to bring truth and justice.

ADONAI

Here we find in the *Sh'ma* a return to the emphasis on God's
mercy. I call this the "sandwich effect."

When disciplining our children, we should first communicate the compassionate and merciful heart of ADONAI, then bring
the truth and justice of *Eloheinu*, and then imitate ADONAI by a
reaffirmation of our personal, loving relationship with them. As
Lamentations 3:23 says, ADONAI's grace and compassion "are new
every morning! How great is your faithfulness!"

Echad (One)

The *Sh'ma* is a call to worship one (*echad*) God—ADONAI. It also
informs us that God is a composite unity (*echad*). Our relationships are to reflect this unity or oneness that exist within God
himself. Yeshua's heartfelt prayer in John 17:20–23 speaks of this
unity:

> I pray not only for these, but also for those who will trust in
> me because of their word, that they may all be one. Just as
> you, Father, are united with me and I with you, I pray that
> they may be united with us, so that the world may believe
> that you sent me. The glory which you have given to me, I
> have given to them; so that they may be one, just as we are
> one–I united with them and you with me, so that they may
> be completely one, and the world thus realize that you sent
> me, and that you have loved them just as you have loved me.

Clearly, one of Yeshua's primary desires for us is that we would
be one as he and the Father are one. This includes our relationships
with our children. Our prayer should be that our children would
walk in fellowship with us and with God–that we and our children
would be "one" and that they would be "one" with God.

God has a purpose for this unity. God's aim for our relationships is that we would be one so that the world may be reached
with Messiah. It is a powerful witness to the world to see a family
walking in biblical unity.

This oneness of fellowship is a very important theme in John's writings. 1 John 1:7 says, "But if we are walking in the light, as he is in the light, then we have fellowship with each other, and the blood of his Son Yeshua purifies us from all sin." To be able to have honest communication–to know and to be known–is one of our greatest needs. I enjoy walks with my wife, Silvia. And when our conversations express a depth of openness, we grow closer. We experience that spiritual oneness that God desires for each of us.

There is a great need for parents to truly know their children, particularly in the teenage years. May we seek to cultivate this relationship of openness and oneness with our children throughout their lives. Let us learn from the *Sh'ma*.

Chapter Fifteen

Learning From the Biblical Festivals

W HEN THE LORD COMMANDED his people to celebrate his festivals, he knew that doing so would help them to remember his Word and incorporate godly principles into their way of life. Although this discussion is in no way exhaustive of the festivals of Israel, I want to share some exciting ways that we can teach our children through them.

Shabbat, the Sabbath

After God created the world, he rested on the seventh day. Genesis 2:3 says, "God blessed the seventh day and separated it as holy; because on that day God rested from all his work which he had created." In Exodus 20:8, God told his people to "Remember the day, Shabbat, to set it apart for God." The Sabbath meal on Friday evening is a tradition that has helped the Jewish people maintain their unique identity throughout history. It is also a reminder of God's covenant with them, and the order of Creation.

At Ets Chaiyim (Tree of Life) School, we welcome Shabbat on Friday afternoons with our Kabbalat Shabbat service. As the students participate in the lighting of the Sabbath candles, as well as the blessings over the bread and wine, they learn biblical principles.

As we enjoy Sabbath rest, we grow in our relationship with the Lord of the Sabbath. Yeshua said, "Come to me, all of you who are struggling and burdened, and I will give you rest. Take my yoke upon you and learn from me, because I am gentle and humble in heart, and you will find rest for your souls. For my yoke is easy, and my burden is light" (Matt. 11:28–30). As our children see us walking in the Sabbath rest of Yeshua, we convey a message about trusting him in every aspect of our lives.

Rosh HaShanah, the Head of the Year

Leading up to *Yom Kippur* is *Yom Teruah*, the Day of Blowing (traditionally known as *Rosh Hashanah*), which begins ten days of repentance before God. In our festival service, we blow the *shofar* (ram's horn). This reminds us of the *shofar* blast that will sound when Messiah returns.

In his book *God's Appointed Times*, Barney Kasdan describes the festival as a day of "regathering":

> The purpose of this holy day is summed up in one word–regathering. Since the fall holidays call us to regather to a pure faith in God, Rosh HaShanah has come to represent
> the day of repentance. It is the day when the people of Israel take stock of their spiritual condition and make the necessary changes to insure that the upcoming new year will be pleasing to God. (Kasdan, 64)

Because *Rosh HaShanah* begins the fall festivals, it has become known as the spiritual head of the year. The blessing of the new year is commemorated by eating various sweet foods. At Ets Chaiyim School, the students enjoy eating apples dipped in honey to celebrate this day. Tasting sweet foods on *Rosh HaShanah* leaves a lasting impression on our children.

Yom Kippur, the Day of Atonement

We can teach our children much about the atoning work of Yeshua through *Yom Kippur.* Leviticus 23:27–28 says,

> The tenth day of this seventh month is Yom Kippur; you are to have a holy convocation, you are to deny yourselves, and you are to bring an offering made by fire to ADONAI. You are not to do any kind of work on that day, because it is Yom Kippur, to make atonement for you before ADONAI your God.

In biblical times, this was the day when the high priest would enter the Most Holy Place with sacrificial blood to make atonement for the people. Yeshua, through his death, made a way for all who trust in him to boldly enter God's presence.

As we approach this day, we have an excellent opportunity to call our children to a lifestyle of turning from sin and receiving forgiveness through Yeshua, as the writer to the Hebrews wrote:

> So, brothers, we have confidence to use the way into the Holiest Place opened by the blood of Yeshua. He inaugurated it for us as a new and living way through the *parokhet* [dividing wall], by means of his flesh. We also have a great *cohen* [priest] over God's household. Therefore, let us approach the Holiest Place with a sincere heart, in the full assurance that comes from trusting–with our hearts sprinkled clean from a bad conscience and our bodies washed with pure water. (Hebrews 10:19–22)

Yom Kippur reminds us that we should not expect sinless perfection from our children. Instead, we should teach them to lay hold of Yeshua's cleansing blood and renewing power by repentance and confession of sin: "If we acknowledge our sins, then, since he is trustworthy and just, he will forgive them and purify us from all wrongdoing" (1 John 1:9).

My father taught me that when I am caught in a fault, instead of getting defensive, I should acknowledge the fault and the blame will cease. As long as we deny our sin, the blame does not go away. "If we claim not to have sin, we are deceiving ourselves, and the truth is not in us" (1 John 1:8). But as soon as we willingly and fully acknowledge our sin, the blame stops. We can help our children learn to quickly confess their sin when they miss the mark. This character quality will help them to prosper in life as they learn to walk under authority, especially with teachers and employers. The ten days from *Rosh Hashanah* to *Yom Kippur* are ideal times to teach self-examination, which leads to repentance and peace with God through Yeshua.

Sukkot, the Festival of Tabernacles

Sukkot (Booths), or the Festival of Tabernacles, is an eight-day celebration of the harvest. In Leviticus 23:42–43, the Lord called the Israelites to live in booths "so that generation after generation of you will know that I made the people of Isra'el live in *sukkot* when I brought them out of the land of Egypt" (Lev. 23:43). The *sukkah*, a small hut or booth, is a wonderful tool for teaching children. In the home, the congregation, and the school, the image of the *sukkah* helps our children remember and understand that the Jewish people lived in temporary dwellings after leaving Egypt.

From another perspective, "the sukkos referred to in the verse are actually . . . Clouds of Glory, that surrounded and protected the Jewish people from the elements throughout their forty-year wandering in the wilderness" (Cohen, 157). Celebrating *Sukkot* helps our children learn to abide in the blessing of God's covering and protection over every area of their lives.

Psalm 100:4 tells us to "enter his gates with thanksgiving, enter his courtyards with praise; give thanks to him, and bless his name." Giving thanks is a way of entering into God's presence and becoming closer to the Lord. We can use the appointed time of *Sukkot* to inspire in our children an attitude of thanksgiving! As the holiday, *Sukkot*, comes during the time of the fall harvest, we can make *sukkot* (booths) with all kinds of colorful fruits and vegetables. Through this, our children can learn to give thanks to God for his provision, including our food and shelter.

Moreover, parents can use *Sukkot* as a time to teach children that all nations will one day come together to celebrate the Festival of Tabernacles in the Messianic Kingdom. As Zechariah 14:16 says, "Finally, everyone remaining from all the nations that came to attack Yerushalayim [Jerusalem] will go up every year to worship the king, ADONAI-*Tzva'ot*, and to keep the festival of *Sukkot*."

Finally, the Festival of Tabernacles points to the incarnation. John 1:14 says, "The Word became flesh and made his dwelling among us." The phrase "made his dwelling," relates to the word for tabernacle. Yeshua "tabernacled among us then, and he will tabernacle among us again in the Messianic age. The celebration of the Festival of Booths celebrates the Messiah who once tabernacled among us, now tabernacles within us, and in the future will again tabernacle among us" (Lancaster, 97). The Festival of *Sukkot* reminds children that Yeshua is always with them.

Purim, the Festival of Lots

Purim is a time to remember the events described in the book of Esther. As we know, God has been faithful to preserve the Jewish people, from the evil plot of Haman to Hitler's gas chambers. *Purim* is a time to celebrate "the days on which the Jews obtained rest from their enemies and the month which for them was turned from sorrow into gladness and from mourning into a holiday; they were to make them days of celebrating and rejoicing, sending portions [of food] to each other and giving gifts to the poor" (Esther 9:22). Esther 9:27-28 says that "every generation, every family" would remember this time, and that "all who joined them [the Jews]" would also celebrate.

We can teach our children valuable lessons from the events that occurred during this time. Esther showed godly courage, risk-taking faith, and concern for her people, not selfishness. In our homes, schools, and congregations, our children can joyfully give food to one another and gifts to the poor; they can dress up as different people from the Book of Esther. When children read or perform the *Megillah* (the story of Esther), the drama can make a lasting impression on them. As they act out the various roles, they internalize God's Word. *Purim* is a very festive and educational time.

We can also use the time of *Purim* to remind our children that God has a special plan and purpose for their lives. They have a destiny to fulfill. Esther's uncle, Mordecai, exhorted her to speak up for her people: "Who knows whether you didn't come into your royal position precisely for such a time as this" (Esther 4:14). These words point to Esther's purpose; God used her to save Israel from annihilation.

While growing up, my parents instilled in me a keen sense that God had a special plan for my life. *Purim* can help us as parents communicate the same message to our children.

Pesach, Passover

Passover commemorates how God faithfully brought Israel out of Egypt. In obedience to the Lord's command, the Israelites placed the blood of lambs on the doorframes of their houses so that the angel of death would pass over them and not slay their firstborn. Passover is an excellent opportunity to teach our children about Yeshua's identity as the perfect Passover Lamb. As we apply the blood of Yeshua to our hearts in faith, and repent of our sins, the Lord forgives our sins. He "passes over" them.

The Passover *seder* is an excellent way to learn about God and what he has done in history. The many symbols and the four questions that the child asks (with the answers typically provided by the father) reflect textbook teaching methods.

At the Passover table, children learn by tasting different foods. One such food is *matzah* (unleavened bread). The Israelites ate unleavened bread because they had to leave Egypt in haste. Through eating *matzah* and removing leaven from our homes, we can explain to our children the importance of getting rid of all sin from our lives (1 Cor. 5:6-13).

We can make it our goal to enjoy Passover with our children. Through the *seder*, we can remember God's deliverance of Israel from Egypt and his deliverance of mankind from sin and death through Yeshua.

Celebrating the Lord's festivals is an outstanding way of teaching our children lasting biblical principles and pointing them to the Lord in a way that can capture their imagination for a lifetime.

Part Three

The Stages of Child Development

NOW THAT WE HAVE DISCUSSED practical parenting methods for the training and instruction of our children, we will address the different stages of child development from a biblical perspective—the infant stage, the child stage, and the youth stage.

Because this section deals with children at different stages, there will be some overlap by necessity. Many methods of training and instruction are applicable throughout childhood into the teenage years. However, there are clear differences between the infant and the child and between the child (up to about age 12) and the youth (the teenage years). Although the growth and development of each child is unique, I will put forward general biblical expectations for our children's behavior at different stages.

Chapter Sixteen

The Infant Stage

J EREMIAH 1:5 READS, "Before I formed you in the womb, I knew you; before you were born, I separated you for myself. I have appointed you to be a prophet to the nations." God knew our children before they were conceived; he designed them with purposes in mind (Ps. 139:16). We need to recognize the precious gifts of life that we have stewardship over and, from the time they are in the womb, seek to raise our children to follow the Lord.

The Baby in the Womb

We can establish a healthy beginning for our developing babies in the womb. One way is to pray daily for them, talking to them and speaking Scripture over them. Our home atmosphere should be a place of peace. We should seek to build a home of harmony, avoiding harsh arguing. Praise and worship music can be played to encourage this sense of peace as well.

Once our children's names are decided, we can speak their names as we talk to our babies. I often spoke to our first child when she was in the womb, and when Anna was born, I had a sense that we already had a relationship with each other. On her first day out of the womb, when she was crying in the nursery, I spoke soothingly to her in a similar tone and with similar words of blessing as when she had been in the womb: "Hi, Anna. This is Daddy. Daddy loves you. God bless you." She would quickly calm down at my words. I felt confident that we had developed a relationship from the time she was in Silvia's womb. We already knew and loved each other; we had developed a close bond. When our babies are born, they should already have a sense of belonging in our family and security in our home.

The Child's Name

Naming a child is an important decision. 1 Samuel 1:20 says that Hannah "gave birth to a son, whom she named Sh'mu'el, 'because I asked ADONAI for him.'" Hannah had a very important, God-given reason for the name that she gave to her son. In biblical times, the name was very significant; the name sometimes spoke of the person's character and identity.

It is good to seek the Lord's direction for the names of our children. These names will be spoken over them for their entire lives. With our son Joshua Ezekiel, Silvia and I sought the Lord regarding his name. Joshua means, "The Lord is salvation." He is named after Joshua, who led the Israelites to take the Promised Land. We continually thank God that our son will take the "promised land" that God has for him. In addition, his middle name, Ezekiel, means "strength of God." Our prayer is that Joshua Ezekiel will be a strong, courageous, and compassionate leader who will seek to please God without worrying about what others think of him.

A child's name can be very significant. It can speak of the child's identity and can be a key factor in how he views himself for the duration of his life.

The Parent-Infant Relationship

The most important thing we can do with our babies is establish a delightful, loving relationship with them. When Anna was eight weeks old, I came home from work and spent time with her. I was talking to her, asking her all kinds of questions, and saying "Hi" to her over and over. Well, she tried so hard to talk with me–putting her tongue out, moving her face, and breathing excitedly. She cooed and said, "Hooroo." Finally she started crying out of frustration; she wanted to talk with me but couldn't. I told her, "It's OK. You don't have to talk."

Through this experience, I saw that Anna wanted to talk with me and imitate me. Indeed, God has placed in our infants a natural desire to connect to us. We have a wonderful opportunity to communicate our great pleasure.

Babies begin their lives completely dependent on us, particularly on mothers. They need constant care and seem to demand immediate fulfillment of their wants. Infants build a sense of trust through breast feeding, a method designed by God. Psalm 8:2 provides an illustration of the strength-building activity of breast-feeding: "From the mouths of babies and infants at the breast you established strength because of your foes, in order that you might silence the enemy and the avenger."

The father's presence is also instrumental to a baby's development. Hosea 11:3–4, which speaks of our Father's love toward his child Ephraim, gives a picture of a daddy's involvement:

> Yet it was I who taught Efrayim to walk; I took them by their arms. But they did not know that it was I who was healing them, who was guiding them on through human means with reins made of love. With them I was like someone removing the yoke from their jaws, and I bent down to feed them.

Dads should never think that they have a limited role in the life of their infants. They can help with their feeding, change their diapers, provide love to them, connect with them, play with them, talk with them, and help them crawl and walk. There is much physical effort needed to take care of a baby. It is definitely a task requiring teamwork between the mother and the father.

The Scriptures describe weaning as a key point in the life of a child. 1 Samuel 1:21–23 speaks of Hannah's nursing of her son Samuel until he was weaned:

> The husband, Elkanah, went up with all his household to offer the yearly sacrifice to ADONAI and fulfill his vow. But Hannah did not go up, explaining to her husband, "Not till the child has been weaned. Then I will bring him, so that he can appear before ADONAI and live there forever." Her husband Elkanah answered her, "Do what seems good to you; stay here until you have weaned him. Only may ADONAI bring about what he said." So the woman stayed behind and nursed the child, until she weaned him.

During the first few years of life, basic trust is established and the foundation for a positive relationship between baby and mother is built. Both parents should make maximum use of the early years to establish strong relationships with their baby. Psalm 131:2 speaks of the peace of a weaned child: "But I have stilled and quieted my soul; like a weaned child with its mother, like a weaned child is my soul within me."

Training Our Infants

Once infants have successfully learned to receive feeding, we should begin to move toward a schedule of feedings and naps. By doing so they are being trained from the very beginning, trained to fit into the life of the family instead of needing to be the center of attention. While the mother provides the baby's nourishment, he learns to fall asleep on his own and trust that his needs will be met. We should not give into our babies' demands while, at the same time, being sensitive to provide for their needs. Each of our four babies was sleeping through the night by eight weeks old. Silvia and I are convinced that the reason for this is that we established a routine of feedings and naps throughout the day.

While recognizing that our children are created in the image of God, we need to be aware that our precious little ones also come to us with a certain innate nature. Psalm 51:5 says, "Surely I was sinful at birth, sinful from the time my mother conceived me." Psalm 58:3 expresses the point even more graphically: "Even from birth the wicked go astray; from the womb they are wayward and speak lies." None of us want to think of our newborns as "wicked"; however, we do need to understand that our children will seek to exert their own will from the very beginning.

Parents need to be parents; we need to understand that we are in charge, not our babies. As our infants develop and exert their own will, we need to direct and control them. When our infants throw temper tantrums, we should not give in to them. Instead, we should gently provide control and thereby make our babies obey, whether we are changing a diaper or bathing them. Our baby crying noisily is not grounds for stopping our activity to appease him.

To establish parental control, infants should be trained to respond to the parent's command, especially "No." They can also learn to respond to commands such as "Stop" and "Come," which serve a protective function. As these commands are established, we create boundaries within which our children are allowed to explore. For example, our babies can learn to play in the family room while being trained not to touch the television.

Proverbs 22:15 says, "Folly is bound up in the heart of a child, but the rod of discipline will drive it far from him." We need to work hard to counter our babies' self-oriented nature; they learn to be good through discipline. For the six-month-old infant, we can use pain in a controlled way to require obedience to the command, "No." For example, the parent can press the baby's hand firmly when he throws food. This trains the infant that "No" means he is not allowed to throw food. While we should not spank until after the baby is about twelve months old, we can squeeze the hand to provide discipline and to help our infant understand what "No" means.

Instructing Our Infants

Our babies learn much through their exploratory play. They need to be stimulated to experience their environment. As they grow older and start to move around, they are searching, looking, learning, and becoming fascinated with their surroundings.

During the child's first fifteen months (infancy), the mother should seek to develop her child's independence to the maximum. The infant's natural curiosity drives him to learn, adding to his knowledge in an ever-increasing way.

When my daughter was about fourteen months old, she desired to walk and explore her surroundings. Silvia and I would watch her walking from a safe distance. Anna would talk loudly, point, and joyfully walk as fast as she could. She just loved her new-found ability to walk and explore. As she interacted with others, she seemed to be a leader, full of courage and seemingly ready to command her troops with full determination and purpose!

Paul knew that Timothy had been taught from infancy:

> But as for you, continue in what you have learned and have become convinced of, because you know those from whom you learned it, and how *from infancy you have known the holy Scriptures*, which are able to make you wise for salvation through faith in Messiah Yeshua. (2 Timothy 3:14–15, italics added)

Timothy had the Scriptures read to him from a young age, probably from his first days. Likewise, our babies can begin to know God's Word.

A major tool is reading to our infants, including directly from the Scriptures. Bible storybooks with pictures will stimulate and establish a strong interest in God's Word from an early age. We should make reading books with stimulating story lines and strong character-building themes a regular part of our instructional strategy with both infants and children. Stories have a powerful way of reaching the hearts of children. Taking the time to discuss the themes internalizes godly values.

When our daughter was seven months old, she became quite animated when we read her a picture book. Both during the reading and after, she talked very excitedly. It was obvious that she was fully engaged in the book's content and enjoyed the pictures, responding with baby talk. It is a great pleasure and privilege to see our infants learn right before our eyes!

God has given our babies the gift of language. They desire to communicate with us. They have a natural ability to develop language capacity. However, sometimes infants can become frustrated because they cannot communicate their needs. Before they are able to use intelligible words, we can instruct them to use sign language. We can teach them various signs for "mommy," "daddy," "thank you," "more please," and "I'm sorry."

Our babies also learn from the positive spiritual health of the family. Joel 2:15–16 speaks of how babies were included in a sacred assembly: "'Blow the shofar in Tziyon! Proclaim a holy fast, call for a solemn assembly.' Gather the people; consecrate the congregation; assemble the leaders; gather the children, even infants sucking at the breast." Our infants can be a part of worshipping the Lord.

Anna was thirteen months old when she lifted up her hands and clapped to praise Yeshua during times of worship. Sometimes, when she heard music, she would automatically lift her hands as if she thought that the purpose of music was to praise Yeshua. Children, beginning in their infancy, can see that the true purpose of music is indeed to praise ADONAI.

In our home, we have played upbeat praise music with our young children and have spent joyous times together praising the Lord. We like to march around the living room and dining room table, clapping and waving our hands, and sometimes using instruments, as we enthusiastically praise God. My young son Nehemiah enjoys taking turns with his siblings leading the rest of us in praising God as we march (and sometimes run) around the living and dining rooms. Our relationship with the Lord, our attitudes, and our demeanor all contribute to a spiritually uplifting home atmosphere, a major factor in instructing our little ones.

Chapter Seventeen

The Child Stage

AS SOON AS an infant begins to exert his own will, he can be considered a child. The child stage continues up through about age twelve. In discussing the parent-child relationship, I will provide specific pointers for dealing with our children as toddlers (fifteen to thirty-six months), preschoolers (ages three to six), and elementary school age children (six to twelve).

Our children have an intrinsic desire to please us. They want to know that we are delighted with them. Because a young child's relationship with his father helps to form his perspective of his heavenly father, God, we need to be responsive.

Of course no father is as perfect as God; however, as fathers, we need to imitate our heavenly father through the constancy of our love, by providing clear boundaries, and by communicating acceptance, instead of criticism. By walking in these ways, we help our children gain a balanced view of our God, one who is both loving and just in all his ways.

As our child enters the elementary years, the relationship between father and son, mother and daughter, are critical. The son should spend time doing things with his father, learning to identify with him in the process. Likewise, the daughter should build a strong identification with her mother.

The preceding point assumes that both parents are in the home. The biblical design is for two committed parents to be in the home for the benefit of the children. Many of the ills in our society can be attributed to the breakdown of the familial structure in the home. Yeshua himself pleaded regarding the important oneness of the husband and wife relationship: "Therefore what God has joined together, let man not separate" (Mark 10:9).

Our marriage covenant is absolutely critical to the healthy development of our children. Husbands and wives need to guard their hearts toward each other. Husbands particularly need to avoid the harshness of voice and action that can rip a family apart. Otherwise, violence will resound in the hearts of our children. We must realize that the quality of our relationships with our children is intrinsically tied to the quality of our relationship with each other as husband and wife.

However, the reality is that many children do not have both parents living with them. In this situation, steps need to be taken for the sake of the child's well being. Psalm 68:5 encourages those who have no father that God will be "a father to the fatherless." As a principal, I have witnessed a number of situations in which godly adults have stepped into a child's life when one or both biological parents have abdicated their responsibility. And I have observed that God, through his healing mercy, has redeemed the lives of young people in very difficult family situations.

We must never forget that God has given us the authority necessary for our parental task. In our relationship with our children, we are first and foremost our children's parents. We should resist the urge to be our child's "buddy," in an immature, even selfish way. In order to be effective, we must provide external control of our children until they develop the internal controls to walk in obedience.

During the child stage, the emphasis is on providing loving and consistent disciplinary training to our children. Proverbs 3:11–12 says, "My son, don't despise ADONAI's discipline or resent his reproof; for ADONAI corrects those he loves like a father who delights in his son." Parents who love and delight in their children will be faithful to discipline their children so they can succeed in life. As previously discussed, our children have a nature which can cause them to be self-centered. Our children will naturally do what they want to do. Parents must control this tendency.

Until an internal control (faith) is established in our children, they are under the law of their parents. During the child stage, the emphasis should be on *what* to do. Keep it simple. We should tell our children exactly what to do and teach our children a simple biblical truth that provides the reason for right behavior.

If trained properly, consistent obedience should normally occur between ages eight and twelve. In our children's training, chastisement is frequently necessary. If our children need spankings because they are rebelling, throwing a temper, or have hurt someone physically, then we should administer the needed discipline. On the other hand, we need to avoid threatening our children with discipline, like spankings, at some future time. These idle threats diminish the child's respect for the parent and make him more willing to disobey again, especially if the threats are never meted out.

If our child has a habit of lying to authorities, we need to find out why. Perhaps it is due to how we react to him when he does something wrong. It is important that we avoid harsh "I-need-my-child-to-be-perfect" reactions in which our child feels shamed before us and/or others if he ever does something wrong and it comes to our attention. If we do react harshly often enough, we will end up negatively training our child to lie, simply to avoid our wrath.

The question for us is, "Do we have a truly trusting relationship with our children?" We should not fall for the "quality time versus quantity time" argument when it comes to spending time with our children. Both are needed. As our children get older and have more outside influences in their lives, we can ask ourselves: "Do we know our children? Do our children desire us to know them? Do they know us? Is our relationship characterized by open communication?" We should not make any assumptions regarding what may or may not be happening in our children's hearts or minds. We need to *know* what is going on in their lives.

God calls us to be consistent examples of Yeshua to our children, "full of grace and truth" (John 1:14). We will never be perfect examples of Yeshua. Nevertheless, we should consistently walk in that balance of grace and truth, as we build a close and trusting relationship with our children.

Parents with several children inevitably have to face the issue of sibling rivalry. Often this issue comes to the forefront when our children are tattling on each other. We need to be proactive with our children regarding this; otherwise we will become exhausted dealing with their accusations and complaints against each other.

With our own children, we have emphasized the need for peace and harmony in the home. I recall my father saying, "No one has the right to upset the peace in the home." The overriding principle is expressed in Ephesians 4:2–3: "Always be humble, gentle and patient, bearing with one another in love, and making every effort to preserve the unity the Spirit gives through the binding power of *shalom*."

We tell our children that they are not to come to us with complaints about their siblings unless they are in an unsafe situation or their sibling continues to physically hurt them after they have "turned the other cheek." We challenge them to be above the fray and that "it is their glory to overlook an offense" (Prov. 19:11). Our strategy is to teach them to bear with each other, to overlook offenses, to seek to work things out in a way pleasing to the Lord without their parents' assistance.

If our children are unwilling to resolve the conflict among themselves, they are separated into different rooms. Sooner or later, they desire contact with their siblings, not isolation. The condition for coming out of their room is that they are willing to work things out in a peaceful manner.

Our children should learn responsibility, including daily and weekly household chores. The use of a chart of tasks provides them with a way to build "precept upon precept." We can have our children focus on two to five jobs at a time, depending on their age. Parents can give a star for the successful completion of tasks, such as making their bed, cleaning their room, and clearing the table. This way they gain a sense of responsibility for their contributions to the management of the home.

Toddlers (Fifteen to Thirty-Six Months)

Genesis 33:13–14 speaks of the tenderness of children, who move at a slower pace than adults. We should not drive our children harshly, but lead them with tenderness.

The toddler stage is critical for building personal confidence and taking initiative. If the mother is overbearing, the toddler will be hindered in developing self-confidence. We need to have realistic expectations of them. Many first-born children develop perfectionist tendencies because of the unrealistic expectations of inexperienced parents. Instead of focusing on our child being perfect, we should focus on building up our child's self esteem through communicating much favor to him. This doesn't mean that we let down in providing consistent training; it just means that while we train, we also lavish much favor and build up their confidence.

A major aspect of loving our toddlers is providing consistent training through proper control. The many proverbs on the use of the rod take on special significance during this period. Boundaries and limit setting are critical. If our toddler openly rebels, he should receive a quick spanking with the rod.

We need a devotional atmosphere in the home. We should not let questionable television programs and music fill the hearts and minds of our children. Instead, we should spend time reading Bible stories with pictures to our children and other character-building stories.

Providing our toddler with opportunities to socialize with other children will guide their development. At two years old, they have sufficient basic trust to develop social relationships with other children. They should be required to share their toys when playing with peers and siblings. This is because the foundations for principles of unselfishness, sharing, and the detrimental results of stealing, are established in the toddler stage. Modeling sharing behavior before our children, as well as praising them for sharing, are great ways to train toddlers. When our toddler grabs a toy from someone's hands, he should receive a quick physical reminder that this is not acceptable behavior.

Preschoolers (Ages Three to Six)

A continued emphasis on discipline, including control and chastisement, is necessary. At age three or four, children express anger by throwing temper tantrums. We must restrain these displays of anger. It is critical that we not give in to these demonstrations. If children find that they can get their way, they will think that throwing temper tantrums is effective and grow up using them to gain their desires. We should expect the possibility of conflict when our children do not get their way. We must win these battles so our preschoolers are trained properly.

Isaiah 28:9–10 is applicable to the instruction of both our toddlers and preschoolers:

> Who is it he is trying to teach? To whom is he explaining his message? To children weaned from their milk, to those just taken from the breast? For it is: Do and do, do and do, rule on rule, rule on rule; a little here, a little there.

This passage shows how to begin to instruct our preschoolers, ones just weaned—being repetitive, letting each rule support and confirm the rules that came before it. We are to instruct our preschoolers step-by-small-step, in an incremental way. We will often feel like our work is three steps forward, and two steps back. I know my wife often felt this way while toilet training our children. However, we will reap the reward if we do not give up!

Preschoolers need help learning how to take care of themselves. They should be allowed increasing independence in feeding themselves, putting on their clothes, and becoming completely toilet trained. In addition, when our children are about four, we can give them short Scripture verses to memorize.

The first six years of our children's lives are particularly critical. Yeshua made clear the importance he placed on little children:

People were bringing children to him so that he might touch them, but the *talmidim* [disciples] rebuked those people. However, when Yeshua saw it, he became indignant and said to them, "Let the children come to me, don't stop them, for the Kingdom of God belongs to such as these. Yes! I tell you, whoever does not receive the Kingdom of God like a child will not enter it!" And he took them in his arms, laid his hands on them, and made a *b'rakhah* over [blessed] them. (Mark 10:13–16)

Children are uniquely prepared to enter the Kingdom of God because of their receptivity and faith. By age six, children should be able to experience God's forgiveness through Yeshua: "Yet to all who received him, to those who believed in his name, he gave the right to become children of God" (John 1:12).

When Caleb was four years old, Silvia had a conversation with him that led to his receiving Yeshua as his Savior. Well, he was very excited and called a number of family, friends, and teachers to tell them the news! One of the friends was a three-year-old girl. We later heard that, after this girl had talked with him, her mother explained to her the meaning of Yeshua living in her heart. This girl then invited Yeshua into her life and embraced him as her Savior. Caleb's joy at becoming a child of God and his desire to share the good news with others resulted in the expansion of God's Kingdom in the heart of another child. As parents, we need to be aware of the need to share the good news of Messiah Yeshua with our children when they are young.

The importance of training by age six has been noticed by science. "Many psychiatrists estimate on the basis of their studies that approximately 85 percent of the adult personality is already formed by the time the individual is six years old" (Meier, 45). By showing love and exercising consistent discipline through the first six years of our child's life, we can make it easier on ourselves for the next fourteen years.

The Elementary Years (Ages Six to Twelve)

Sound discipline should be continued in the elementary years. Reproof, the rod if necessary, and matching penalties, should be used. Solomon illustrates the need for quick discipline: "When the sentence for a crime is not quickly carried out, the hearts of the people are filled with schemes to do wrong" (Ecclesiastes 8:11). Since the elementary school child's attention span is relatively short, the penalty for wrongdoing should be carried out quickly.

A stay-at-home mom should not wait for her husband to discipline their children when he gets home. Neither should they be dealt with at some future time (perhaps a restriction of some upcoming activity). These strategies will only build resentment and give the child time to scheme other wrongs, as Solomon indicates, while forgetting the reason for the discipline in the first place. The best method is a quick penalty for the action. The action is forgiven, the discipline is finished quickly, and children are restored fully to family. Soon they will be continuing cheerfully with their day.

We need to remember to be calm and consistent. When parents are inconsistent, it is because they provide "discipline" based on their emotional state. Instead of acting on principle, they tolerate bad behavior in the name of patience. However, eventually they "lose it" and react in harshness. When they react this way, they actually abuse their children verbally and even physically at times. In disciplining our children, we need to communicate calmly. We should never yell at them or shame them. If we are consistent and calm, our children will know what is expected and will be secure within that framework.

Proverbs 6:16–19 lists behaviors that we should teach our children to avoid:

> There are six things ADONAI hates, seven which he detests: a haughty look, a lying tongue, hands that shed innocent blood, a heart that plots wicked schemes, feet swift in running to do evil, a false witness who lies with every breath, and him who sows strife among brothers.

Our children should be expected to respect authority instead of having haughty eyes. They should eschew deception and be held accountable for truth. They should seek to do what is right instead of scheming to do what is wrong. We should emphasize and expect proper manners. They should contribute to a spirit of unity among their siblings, classmates, and neighbors.

Elementary school children sometimes play favorites with their friends, keeping the odd person out. We need to aggressively deal with this tendency as an instance of breaking the Golden Rule. We must resist our natural tendency to take offense on behalf of our children or feel sorry for them at this age. James 3:17–18 says, "But the wisdom from above is, first of all, pure, then peaceful, kind, open to reason, full of mercy and good fruits, without partiality and without hypocrisy. And peacemakers who sow seed in peace raise a harvest of righteousness." Parents who instruct their children according to the Scriptures will emphasize the need to walk in peace and sow peace among others. We need to understand the fact that our children can actually be brutal with each other, cutting each other down, whether they are playing basketball during school recess or riding their bikes in their neighborhood. We should challenge our children to walk in harmony with others and be peacemakers among their neighbors and classmates.

We can use the inevitable trials that children face to develop character: "Consider it pure joy, my brothers, whenever you face trials of many kinds, because you know that the testing of your faith develops perseverance. Perseverance must finish its work so that you may be mature and complete, not lacking anything" (James 1:2-4). If our child is dealing with an overbearing teacher, for example, we can take him out of the class and away from the teacher, or we can see this as an opportunity. We can encourage our child to pray for the person, to respect his authority, to take responsibility for his own behavior, to find ways to serve the teacher, and to win him over with a godly attitude. As our children learn to persevere through these kinds of trials, they gain confidence that they can overcome in all of life.

We can prepare our children to deal with conflict in a covenantal way. Matthew 18:15–16 says:

> If your brother commits a sin against you, go and show him
> his fault–but privately, just between the two of you. If he
> listens to you, you have won back your brother. If he doesn't
> listen, take one or two others with you so that every accu-
> sation can be supported by the testimony of two or three
> witnesses.

When your child is bothered by another child, either verbally
or physically, you can teach him to go with the right attitude and
ask that person to stop what he is doing. If that action does not
solve the problem, your child should be urged to bring someone
else along, perhaps a teacher or a parent, to confront the other
person. If this process is used, your child should not feel he is
being a "tattle tale." He is simply following God's process for
resolving interpersonal conflict. If we teach this very important
skill to our children, they will benefit immensely from it.

At elementary school age, our children generally desire to please
us. Our daily example is increasingly important. Family devotions
should be a regular part of our home life. In these times, we need
to consider the attention span of our children (about five to fifteen minutes) and be creative and spontaneous.

Our children can develop a sincere relationship with the Father;
they can learn to hear the voice of God through reading Scripture
and through quiet times of prayer. We need to encourage these
spiritual activities.

We should take advantage of the increasing academic skills that
our children will be gaining in elementary school. We can encourage our children to start reading healthy books, including daily
Bible reading. We can set up a system of regular memorization of
age-appropriate Scripture passages, giving our children a reward
when they've committed these passages to memory. When I was
a child, my parents had me memorize passages of Scripture and
then recite them to a fellow congregant at services. In this way, the
Word of God was instilled in me from a young age.

Moreover, study skills should be developed, such as regular
drill and review. The importance of completing assignments
needs to be stressed. A daily study time at a designated location

will reinforce the importance of consistency and hard work. We need to work with our children, supporting and challenging them to meet reasonably high expectations as we lay the groundwork for a strong work ethic.

We should provide our children with opportunities to participate with others so they can learn the importance of teamwork. Group games that build trust with others, as well as team sports, can be helpful if the activities are given proper adult guidance. As these areas of character are solidified, our children can be encouraged to develop leadership skills.

Also, education in sexual matters should take place during the elementary school years and it should be done at home. We should answer our children's sex-related questions as they come up in an objective, truthful, and unembarrassed manner.

Influences outside our home should be considered in light of the biblical mandate to teach our children according to God's Word. Our children need to see that our commitment to being part of the Body of Messiah, through the local congregation, is of vital importance in our family life. We should choose a congregation where the Word of God is taught and where we can build strong, covenantal relationships within the family of God. Our children need to see that our commitment to the local congregation is not primarily for us to be served as much as it is to serve the Lord and others. We should train our children to praise the Lord during worship, to listen to the preaching of the Word of God, and to apply the Scriptures to their lives.

In light of the increasing secularization of American schooling, parents should consider home schooling their children. Alternatively, they should consider sending them to a school that integrates the Scriptures into its curriculum, systematically teaches godly character development, and whose teachers both care for the children and provide firm and loving discipline. As an educator, this subject is very close to my heart. So much of our children's waking hours are devoted to school. As we have seen in the *Sh'ma*, God calls us to teach our children all day long according to his Word. Parents need to be aware that schools are no longer neutral places of learning. Many schools have become institutions of secular humanistic indoctrination, often in the name of tolerance. Because children are so impressionable, parents must consider the schooling question prayerfully. Otherwise, their efforts at home may be watered down or even thwarted during the day.

Finally, summer camps with biblical goals can provide children with a focused experience of exciting activities, healthy exercise, and the opportunity to develop friendships while hearing the good news and being challenged in their walk with the Lord. I had many positive experiences at camp. I encountered God through praise and worship and was challenged in my walk with him through strong preaching of the Word. I also received my initial calling from the Lord at camp.

Transition from the Child to the Youth Stage

As children move from the child stage to the youth stage, the emphasis gradually shifts from training and control to instruction and reason. In training and instructing our children, the emphasis is on "what." In training and instructing our youth, the emphasis shifts to "why." Teenagers develop to the point where they are more and more able to understand the reasons behind the standards, and we should take more time explaining the biblical principles for right behavior.

If our children have been trained well in the child stage, they will be able to maturely accept the standards that we have taught them. The standards will become internal to their character and our children will require less and less parental control.

Chapter Eighteen

The Youth Stage

T HE YOUTH, OR TEENAGE STAGE, is from age twelve or thirteen to nineteen or twenty. The developed reasoning abilities of our teenagers enable them to experience a new kind of interaction with their parents and teachers. Luke 2:41–52 provides an excellent illustration of Yeshua's transition to the youth stage:

> Every year Yeshua's parents went to Yerushalayim for the festival of *Pesach*. When he was twelve years old, they went up for the festival, as the custom required. But after the festival was over, when his parents returned, Yeshua remained in Yerushalayim. They didn't realize this; supposing that he was somewhere in their caravan, they spent a whole day on the road before they began searching for him among their relatives and friends. Failing to find him, they returned to Yerushalayim to look for him. On the third day they found him–he was sitting in the Temple court among the rabbis, not only listening to them but also questioning what they said; and everyone who heard him was astonished at his insight and his responses. When his parents saw him, they were shocked; and his mother said to him, "Son! Why

have you done this to us? Your father and I have been terribly worried looking for you!" He said to them, "Why did you have to look for me? Didn't you know that I had to be concerning myself with my Father's affairs?" But they didn't understand what he meant. So he went with them to Natzeret and was obedient to them. But his mother stored up all these things in her heart. And Yeshua grew both in wisdom and in stature, gaining favor both with other people and with God.

At twelve, Yeshua had developed an internal desire to learn from the rabbis. His reasoning capacities were such that he could ask insightful questions and give answers that showed depth of thought. His behavior showed an increasing independence; however, his actions were not rebellious. His independence was born of an increased understanding of his reason for being, his purpose.

At the same time, Yeshua maintained an attitude of obedience and honor toward his parents; he practiced walking under authority. As he lived in these ways as a young man, his wisdom, stature, and favor with God and with others increased greatly.

Parent-Youth Relationship

In Jewish tradition, young people twelve and older are treated according to a different standard. Through the process of bar mitzvah (for young men) and bat mitzvah (for young women), young people move into a new stage of life in which they are given increased responsibility and freedom. The result of this rite of passage is an increasing capacity for dads to talk man-to-man with their sons and moms to talk woman-to-woman with their daughters. There is an important lesson here for parents.

This new developing relationship with our teenagers should be very positive. We can trust and accept our young people. Empathizing with our teenagers will help them to persevere through serious life changes. Here are some "Suggestions for Relating to Teens in a Positive Way":

1. Deal with any problems in private.
2. State what you perceive the problem to be as early as possible.
3. Tell what you are pleased about first. Avoid direct, derogatory language.
4. Deal with specific actions; avoid ascribing motives.
5. Avoid comparing with others.
6. Forget the past and deal with present issues.
7. Deal with only one complaint at a time.
8. Brainstorm options and possible solutions together.
9. Be patient if there is an over-reaction.
10. Give your teens a chance to cope.
11. Be a resource person.
12. Don't freak out the first time they fail.

(Switzer and Switzer, "Parenting Is an Adventure Seminar" 79a)

While communicating love and acceptance, we should make sure that our youth understand the standards. In fact, our relationship with our teenagers should help us be "real" with them regarding unrighteous influences in the world. We can encourage them that there is a way of escape and that they can be examples of righteousness. When we have earned our children's respect, a foundation is laid for receptivity to our counsel, even into the adult years.

Relationship gives us a voice in our young person's life. It enables us to speak truths about personal responsibility, walking in purity, and refusing self-pity, into the lives of our teenagers. One critical area to monitor is online activity. As a principal, I have had to make parents aware of their teenagers' online communications. Many parents have no idea of what their young people are doing on the Internet. However, having a close relationship with our children enables us to talk about this issue as well as the larger question of what it means to follow Yeshua and keep his commandments.

Maintaining Open Communication

It is important that we work hard to maintain open communication with our youth. Amos 3:3 says, "Do two walk together unless they have agreed to do so?" When the young person seems to be withdrawing from the rest of the family, one of the parents needs to take the time to draw out, listen to, and encourage him or her. The father's relationship is particularly important with the daughter, and the mother's relationship with the son. In fact, we can gain a perspective regarding how a young person will ultimately relate to his or her future spouse by the quality of the relationship with the parent of the opposite gender.

Young people are looking for worthy leadership. If they don't find it in their homes, they will look for it elsewhere. We need to stay relevant and influential in the lives of our teenagers. We can focus on the Word of God as the source of our principles for family life rather than battling between our opinions and theirs. At times, we may need to challenge our young people to wrestle with God's Word about an issue instead of wrestling with us. Nevertheless, aside from what their outward appearances may tell us, we are a very important voice in their lives. Be sure to use it! "Even teenagers, despite all their protests to the contrary, appreciate a firm hand. They can be quite disappointed when parents surrender to their demands" (Donin, 62). Your teenagers are looking for leadership and guidance, even if they profess the opposite.

As we are faithful to espouse the Word of God as our guidebook for living, our young people will be influenced to make their choices based on its truths. Contrary to what may be communicated by their body language, what you say to them will generally have more impact than what any other person says to them, particularly if you work hard to be involved in their lives. We can be used by God to speak to our teenager's conscience as they seek to make right decisions.

At the same time, we need to be prepared to receive truth spoken into our own lives by our young people. A son, for instance, reaches a point of brotherhood with his father in which he is able to talk man-to-man with him. In being confronted by his son, a father needs to be open, rather than defensive. We need to allow our young people to confront us. My dad told my brothers and me, "I will know that you have become a man when you can rebuke me without an ounce of tension in your voice." While this statement challenged me to rise up as a man, I have been blessed with a father who has been willing to be confronted by his sons. This kind of reverse accountability calls for great parental humility born out of a desire to have true relationship with one's adult children.

We need to be quick to acknowledge our own faults before our teenagers. At all costs we must avoid pride which keeps us from facing our own sin. If we try to portray perfection, our teens will eventually see our lack of integrity and will become exasperated, losing respect for us. However, if we are humbly willing to acknowledge our own failures, our teenagers will see reality, rather than hypocrisy, in our lives. What's more, the godly standard in our family is then reinforced (even though we may have broken it), and our young people are not left with unanswered questions. As we bring our own sin into the light, fellowship is restored within our family, and our family can then proceed in a positive direction.

However, it is important that our young people be trained in such a way that whatever reverse accountability they provide to their parents is done in an honoring way. The command to honor one's parents is not to be taken lightly and must be kept in mind whenever teenagers confront their parents. Any questioning should be done in a respectful and gentle manner. Rabbi Tzuriel Ta'aseh provides guidance regarding the spirit of this kind of confrontation:

> If one sees a parent committing a sin . . . he must point out
> his parent's error. However, he must not do so in an insulting
> way or by directly challenging the parent. . . . He should . . .
> use an indirect, questioning approach. For example, he
> might say, "Father, I see you are doing such-and-such. Was
> this the Torah's intent? What about the following passage in

the Torah?" He should present the issue as if he is in doubt and questioning, not challenging. (Ta'aseh, 75)

Unfortunately, as a young adult, I lost my composure and even yelled at my father at times. My parents, however, were willing to provide me with much grace and helped me to work through my issues. Today, we have a warm, positive relationship in which there is mutual respect, admiration, and love for one another.

It should be the goal of every youth to conduct himself with the utmost honor toward his father and mother. Young adults, indeed all adults, should remember the sowing and reaping principle of life: the way they treat and honor (or dishonor) their parents will more than likely be repeated by their own children. While all families experience some conflict during the teenage years, parents who have trained their children properly will experience a growing and enriching relationship with their teenagers.

Training Our Youth

With the onset of abstract reasoning in youth, we can communicate more on an adult level with our adolescents. The rod should only be used for exceptional offenses. Gradually, they will better understand the benefits of living according to God's Word.

With increased privilege and freedom comes increased responsibility. 1 Corinthians 13:11 says, "When I was a child, I spoke like a child, thought like a child, argued like a child; now that I have become a man, I have finished with childish ways." We can help our teens understand that this is a time to grow into the responsible young men and women that God is calling them to be. Childish ways should be left behind. An increasing sense of responsibility and maturity should be fostered.

We can also help our young people overcome temptations: "For everyone born of God overcomes the world. This is the victory that has overcome the world, even our faith" (1 John 5:4). Our teenagers need to understand that they can be pure by living according to God's Word and hiding his Word in their hearts, "How can a young man keep his way pure? By living according to your word. I seek you with all my heart; do not let me stray from your commands. I have hidden your word in my heart that I might not sin against you" (Ps. 119:9–11).

For males, often the purity issue is lust of the flesh. For females, often the purity issue is guarding one's heart for out of it are the issues of life (Prov. 4:23). Sadly, some young ladies have missed their father's love; therefore, they look for love and are vulnerable to anyone who takes an interest in them.

Fathers have a key role with both their sons and their daughters. With their sons, fathers need to be honest regarding the struggle with their eyes, sharing how they can overcome the temptation to lust by meditating on God's Word, prayer, and accountability with other men. A father needs to provide his daughter with nurture and attention so his daughter's cup of love is full to the brim! The following exhortation from 1 Peter 5:8–10 should encourage our young people in the midst of the battle:

> Be self-controlled and alert. Your enemy the devil prowls around like a roaring lion looking for someone to devour. Resist him, standing firm in the faith, because you know that your brothers throughout the world are undergoing the same kind of sufferings.
>
> And the God of all grace, who called you to his eternal glory in Messiah, after you have suffered a little while, will himself restore you and make you strong, firm and steadfast.

When I was a young man, I went through what seemed to be a chronic trial. I could not shake a negative pattern of thinking. The Lord gave me the above Scripture one day on my lunch break. From that time forward, whenever I was attacked in that area, I confessed this word with conviction, and God gave me victory.

Our young people have to endure similar struggles and they can learn to overcome through by God's Word to dwell within them. As our teenagers persevere and mature through these times of struggle, they gain confidence in God.

Instructing Our Youth

We must not "relax" during the youth stage. Our position as the primary teachers of our teenagers is exceedingly important. If not taught, young people will gradually replace their parents' influence with influencers outside the home.

Rightly trained teenagers who respect their parents will receive parental instruction that is foundational for life. When our young people respect us, we can teach them to fear God and hate evil. To expand on this point, we should guide our young people. Parents who have the respect of their teenagers will be able to instruct them in the following areas: spiritual life, purity issues, relationships, calling and career, working with coworkers, choosing friends, and marriage. We should allow our teenagers to discuss with us sexual subjects, especially with the parent of the same sex. If our young people do not raise these issues, we should look for opportunities to discuss them. Keeping the communication open in this area will allow us to be an influence for standards of righteous living. This will benefit our teenagers and their future married lives.

Our young people who are committed to following God should develop a devotional life that includes regular prayer and Scripture reading. As stewards of their lives, they have the capacity to take care of themselves and should be expected to do so.

In addition, 1 Peter 2:11 exhorts believers "to abstain from sinful desires, which war against your soul." Our teens need to trust God to provide for all of their needs, including their sexual needs, even as Paul wrote, "God will meet all your needs" (Phil. 4:19). According to God's Word, sexual needs are to be met in the bonds of a life-long marital commitment to a mate. Our young people should understand God's command not to be unequally yoked in marriage: "Do not be yoked together with unbelievers. For what do righteousness and wickedness have in common? Or what fellowship can light have with darkness?" (2 Cor. 6:14).

Our young people have the capability to make life-long decisions during this stage. Proverbs 3:5–6 provides helpful instruction for our young people as they seek God's guidance for their lives: "Trust in ADONAI with all your heart; do not rely on your own understanding. In all your ways acknowledge him; then he will level your paths." Our teenagers have the energy and vision to make a difference in this world. If captured by God during this time, they can have an impact that will last for eternity.

Sometimes, however, in order for our young people to find their way, we need to "let go" of them and allow God to work. We need to let them work through their own doubts and fears. We need to resist the urge to shelter them from the difficulties of life. We need to let our young adults seek God for themselves. For a while, it may seem to us that things are precarious in our teenagers' lives. We need to allow God to bring our young people through life's trials to him.

Hosea 12:2–6 describes a young person wrestling with God:

> ADONAI also has a grievance against Y'hudah;
> he will punish Ya'akov according to his ways
> and pay him back for his misdeeds.
> In the womb he took his brother by the heel;
> in the strength of his manhood he fought with God.
> Yes, he fought with an angel and won;
> he wept and pleaded with him.
> Then at Beit-El he found him,
> and there he would [later] speak with us-
> ADONAI *Elohei-Tzva'ot*;
> ADONAI is his name!
> So you, return to your God;
> hold fast to grace and justice;
> and always put your hope in your God.

We need to allow our teenagers to be chastised by God. Sometimes they will seek to wrestle with family members, including their parents. But as we get out of the way, they ultimately will have no one to wrestle with but God. As they struggle, they will cry out to him. When they come face to face with ADONAI, they learn his name and in the process return to God. Their relationship with him becomes theirs, rather than their parent's. Ultimately, their life is restored as their hope is placed in ADONAI.

In 1 John 4:18 we read that "love that has achieved its goal gets rid of fear." Our young people need to overcome any fear of failure and step out in faith, pursuing opportunities. Granted, there will be times of uncertainty. However, we need to release our young people to the Lord and trust that they will overcome: "Young people, I have written you because you are strong—the Word of God remains in you, and you have overcome the Evil One" (1 John 2:14).

Part Four

Long-Term Vision

AS PARENTS, it is all too easy to get caught up in the daily work of training our children. At times we may wonder if we are even making progress. In the process, we can easily lose vision.

While all parents desire success for their children, if we are going to raise our children according to God's Word, we need to find our motivation in a biblical vision for what our children can become.

As you read this last section, I hope you prayerfully reflect on what your vision is for your children and then take some time to write down your thoughts. My hope is that this section will help you gain a clearer vision for what your children can become and that it will serve to motivate you in this great calling of raising champions for Yeshua!

Chapter Nineteen

Young People Who Remember Their Creator

ECCLESIASTES 12:1 challenges young people to "remember your Creator while you are young, before the evil days come, and the years approach when you will say, 'They no longer give me pleasure.'" During one's youth, a person is able to focus on developing a close relationship with the Lord before facing the pressures of life, such as holding down a good job, paying the bills, and being responsible for others. Indeed, our children's youth is a time of preparation for making many important life-long choices.

Three Life Decisions

My father told me that there are three important decisions one makes in life: your God, your life partner, and your life calling. I have often challenged young people between the ages of twelve and sixteen to consider the next eight years of their life; I ask them how old they will be in eight years. After they do the math and figure out that they will be about twenty to twenty-four years old,

I tell them that the next eight years of their life will likely impact their life more than any other eight-year period.

One might think that it is almost unfair that young people have to make so many major decisions at such a young age. During their youth, they are truly laying a foundation for a life of blessing or a life of cursing. Teenagers need to know this about the choices they make. God gave choices to his people:

> I call on heaven and earth to witness against you today that I have presented you with life and death, the blessing and the curse. Therefore, choose life, so that you will live, you and your descendants, loving ADONAI your God, paying attention to what he says and clinging to him—for that is the purpose of your life! (Deut. 30:19–20)

Whether or not our teenagers remember their Creator in their youth will have a tremendous impact on the decisions they make and the quality of their lives. When our youth remember their Creator, they are able to withstand the inevitable storms of life. A strong faith in God will prepare them to stand through life's trials and responsibilities, including family responsibilities, financial pressures, and job issues.

Proverbs 3:18 emphasizes the importance of godly wisdom in building a strong foundation in one's life: "She is a tree of life to those who grasp her; whoever holds fast to her will be made happy," or "be blessed." We can use the many admonitions from the Proverbs that express the heart of a father to his son, to challenge our children to embrace the Lord and his wisdom.

Young people have an amazing capacity to be radical about life and to give their all for a worthy cause. When our teenagers respond to a call to give up their life for Messiah, let them do so! We may have some trepidation. But we can be comforted knowing that a heart surrendered to God will be led by God. While we provide our young adults with godly counsel, we need to allow God to direct their steps.

Guarding Their Hearts for Their Future in God

Remembering one's Creator means devoting one's heart to the Lord. This passion for God enables our youth to guard their hearts during a very vulnerable period in their lives. When they focus on Yeshua, it helps them to practice moral purity in preparation for a lifetime of love and commitment to their marriage partner. In Proverbs 4:23, the father warns his son, "Above everything else, guard your heart; for it is the source of life's consequences." We need to exhort our teenagers to guard their hearts and to understand that their heart's affections will, in the end, produce the issues of their lives.

Often, if young people's affections are not directed toward the Lord, they end up with broken marriages and ruined homes later in life. In my years as an educator, I have seen the unfortunate destruction that can happen in the lives of young people when they become focused on pursuing boyfriend-girlfriend relationships, rather than guarding their hearts for the Lord.

Proverbs 31:10–11 says, "A wife of noble character who can find? She is worth far more than rubies. Her husband has full confidence in her and lacks nothing of value." As our young people love the Lord with all of their heart and being, God will bless them. We need to encourage them to trust the Lord for their future mate, to know that God's plan is the best for them, and to pray for their future spouse. When God brings that person into their life, it will be as though they have discovered a great treasure.

I once was asked to describe my wife Silvia. I responded by saying that she is like a never-ending treasure, like a chest full of precious stones in which I keep discovering valuable jewels. I am so grateful that my wife guarded her heart during her youth!

Helping Our Youth Remember Their Creator

How can we help our children remember their Creator in the days of their youth? One thing we can do is to carefully watch over and limit the choices made available to them. Matthew 7:13–14 says, "Go in through the narrow gate; for the gate that leads to destruction is wide and the road broad, and many travel it; but it is a narrow gate and a hard road that leads to life, and only a few find it."

Exodus 23:2 offers a powerful argument for resisting negative peer pressure: "Do not follow the crowd when it does what is wrong." My dad taught my brothers and me to pursue righteous alternatives when our neighborhood friends would press us to get involved in wrongdoing. They would pressure us to do some mischief such as ringing the neighbors' doorbells and then running away and hiding. Instead of following our friends, we could say, "No, we'd rather go over here and play football instead."

When young people are pressured by an unrighteous leader to do wrong, the others in the group know it is wrong and are just waiting for someone else to speak up. When someone has the guts to speak up, most young people want to follow and do the right thing. This is particularly important for our children as they enter middle school.

Invariably, we will be faced with pressure ourselves to do what is wrong when it comes to holding our young people to biblical standards. This pressure may come from our own children: "But all the other kids are allowed to do it!" It may even come from adults, even those in our own congregation.

When our young people challenge us with an argument like "the Johnson family is allowed to do it," we need not make any comment about the Johnson family. We simply need to say, as my parents did, "Well, we're the Switzer family, and we do things differently." We can then share with our teens the biblical rationale for our stand. As parents, we need to convince the gainsayers, who may be our own teenagers (Titus 1:9).

Sometimes, parents are fearful of alienating their children or "causing them to rebel" by telling them that they can't do something. In the process, they end up parenting out of fear, rather than faith, allowing their children to do things they know are not good for them. As a principal, I have seen fathers and mothers parent their young people this way. They are motivated to avoid causing their children to rebel. Instead of standing up in faith and being a person worth emulating, they abdicate their role and give in to their teenagers' wishes. They start allowing them to be involved in questionable activities, ones that in their heart of hearts they know are not the right path for them. In the end, as the Scriptures tell us, that wide path leads to destruction (Matt. 7:13).

We need to be parents worth respecting, leaders worth following. It is imperative that we are real with our children and walk with them. We should not abdicate our rightful role; we need to walk that much closer with our teenagers. We need to be in their lives and be the ones that are there to listen to them. When the opportunity arises, we will be there to provide strong fathering and mothering through speaking truth as well.

In the account of Abraham and Isaac journeying to Mount Moriah, twice the passage says, "and they both went on together" (Gen. 22:6, 8). The picture of father and son walking together is noteworthy: If we are walking with our young people in a trusting relationship, we won't have to parent out of fear; the relationship that we have built will enable us to walk in faith, just as Abraham did. God commended Abraham for this faith.

Keep the faith, speak the truth in love without legalism, and make the path narrow for your youth. Limit their choices and provide righteous alternatives. We can help our teenagers understand that there is a path to destruction and a path to life, and that out of love for them we are seeking to guide them on the narrow path of life. We are to be parents who closely care for the spiritual welfare of our children–especially in their teenage years–so that they may walk in the life-long blessing of being ones who remember their Creator in their youth!

Chapter Twenty

Servant Leaders

WHAT MOTIVATES ME AS A PARENT is the vision of my children one day being servant leaders of godly influence in their families, in their congregations, and in their communities, vessels used by God to advance his Kingdom. We need to challenge our children to follow Yeshua as the ultimate leader, who led through love, servanthood, and courage.

Yeshua: The Ultimate Example of Servant Leadership

Exodus 15:13 gives insight into how the Lord leads: "In your love, you led the people you redeemed; in your strength, you guided them to your holy abode." Far from ruling with an iron fist, the Messiah chose to lead through love and to ask his followers to respond in a relationship of love (John 15:9-17).

Closely related to love is service. Yeshua expressed the importance of servant leadership in Matthew 20:25–28:

> You know that among the Goyim [nations], those who are supposed to rule them become tyrants, and their superiors become dictators. Among you, it must not be like that. On the contrary, whoever among you wants to be a leader

must become your servant, and whoever wants to be first must
be your slave! For the Son of Man did not come to be served,
but to serve–and to give his life as a ransom for many.

What is greatness? Being a professional athlete? Winning the
best actress award at the Oscars? Being a successful politician?
Our task is to help our young people understand that to be great
in God's eyes, they need to be servant leaders. Our challenge is to
teach our children that true greatness is found in servanthood.

Galatians 5:13–14 says, "For, brothers, you were called to be
free. Only do not let that freedom become an excuse for allowing
your old nature to have its way. Instead, serve one another in love.
For the whole of the Torah is summed up in this one sentence:
'Love your neighbor as yourself.'" Being free is not s license to
sin, but being unfettered to bless others. We need to inspire in
our children a sense that God has freed them from being shackled
or weighed down. They are free to be a blessing, to serve God
wholeheartedly, to serve others.

Yeshua led by example. He served. He washed the feet of his
disciples. He cared for their needs. Our Messiah is the Good
Shepherd who gives up his life for his sheep (John 10), and we
should continually affirm him before our children as an example
of how we should lead, serve, and care for others. To help our
children grow up to reach out to that one person who may be
hurting and alone, that is true greatness.

The Scriptures say that he who is faithful in small things will be
faithful in larger things. We need to help our children understand
that if they want to advance in work, in leadership, and in the
Kingdom of God, they need to find something to do and be faithful at it. I told the young men at my school that if they want to
advance in their workplace, they should simply be faithful at what
they have been given to do. They need to make sure their boss can
count on them; then when their boss has a bigger job and needs
someone he can rely on, he will think of them. Eventually they
will be promoted.

We should encourage our children to take whatever gifts God
has given them and use them to serve others. As our young men

and women are faithful in small matters, God will put them in charge of bigger things.

The Scriptures tell us that we—both adults and children—can avoid evil by doing good. Perhaps our young adult is troubled by a besetting sin or is paralyzed by weakness. We should help him to do something good; instead of focusing on the problem, he can do something positive instead.

In my work as a principal and camp director, I have seen first hand the tremendous impact that young people can have on their peers and on younger children when they serve. It is important to provide youth with opportunities to exercise servant leadership. Helping young people prepare for youth conferences, having them carry the weight of responsibility, and then taking the time to debrief with them afterwards, are valuable learning experiences for them.

As our children apply the Word of God through experience, they learn important lessons from both their successes and their failures. Teenagers can be challenged to share the Word, to testify about what God has done in their lives, to minister through drama, to participate on worship teams, to pray for others, and to use their God-given creativity to minister the life of Yeshua to others. "It is good for a man to bear the yoke from his youth" (Lam. 3:27).

The Challenge to Be Courageous

When God called Joshua to lead the Israelites, he commanded him to be a leader full of courage and to follow God's Word in every aspect of his mission. God gave Joshua a vision to lead his people in taking the Promised Land:

> Be strong and courageous, because you will lead these people to inherit the land I swore to their forefathers to give them. Be strong and very courageous. Be careful to obey all the law my servant Moses gave you; do not turn from it to the right or to the left, that you may be successful wherever you go. Do not let this Book of the Law depart from

your mouth; meditate on it day and night, so that you may be careful to do everything written in it. Then you will be prosperous and successful. Have I not commanded you? Be strong and courageous. Do not be terrified; do not be discouraged, for the Lord your God will be with you wherever you go. (Josh. 1:6–9)

God knew that Joshua was going to face many difficulties and would therefore need courage.

We can help our teens exercise courage as they learn to be leaders who take the "promised land" for God's Kingdom. A sense of God's destiny in their lives will help them step out in courageous faith. "For God gave us a Spirit who produces not timidity, but power, love and self-discipline" (2 Tim. 1:7).

God gave Joshua a manual, the Book of the Law, to guide his actions as a leader. As our teenagers meditate on God's Word and allow biblical principles to guide them, they will learn to stand for God, not looking to the right or to the left, as they relate to their peers. When a peer tries to influence them to compromise their principles, they will have the inner strength to lead in a different and godly direction. No matter what they encounter, our young people need not be terrified or discouraged. As children of God, they can lead with confidence in the knowledge that God is with them.

Taking Action

After receiving the LORD's command, Joshua responded with action:

So Joshua ordered the officers of the people: "Go through the camp and tell the people, 'Get your supplies ready. Three days from now you will cross the Jordan here to go in and take possession of the land the LORD your God is giving you for your own.'" (Josh. 1:10–11)

Joshua communicated a vision that motivated the people to action. He delegated responsibility to the officers. The LORD was giving Israel the land, and Joshua was not hesitant to possess it. Whether it is in a classroom, on an athletic team, or on a worship team, our young people have opportunities to communicate vision that motivates people to action.

Nehemiah is another example of a leader who took action. God used him to inspire the people to rebuild the wall of Jerusalem in fifty-two days. Nehemiah provided both practical and spiritual leadership:

> So in the lower parts of the space behind the wall, I stationed men according to their families, with their swords, spears and bows. After inspecting them, I stood up and addressed the nobles, leaders and the rest of the people: "Don't be afraid of them! Remember ADONAI, who is great and fearful; and fight for your brothers, sons, daughters, wives and homes." (Neh. 4:13–14)

Nehemiah took action and inspired the people to remember their God and to fight for their families and children.

Parents have an important calling in the lives of their children. We need to lift up the example of Yeshua, and of leaders such as Joshua and Nehemiah, to inspire our young people to be servant leaders of godly influence in their generation, even if the world around them seems to be going the opposite way.

Conclusion

PARENTS, WE NEED TO WALK SECURELY in our God-given authority to train and instruct our children. As we embrace biblical values to train up our children, and implement biblical parenting methods on a daily basis, we can be confident that we are doing everything we can to see our children live for the Lord. We need to trust God for the ability to parent our children from infancy, into childhood, and through their youth.

Let us persevere in this great call of parenting our children. I believe this passage from Hebrews 10:35–36 offers us encouragement:

> So do not throw away your confidence; it will be richly rewarded. You need to persevere so that when you have done the will of God, you will receive what he has promised.

As the parents of four children, Silvia and I know first hand the daily challenges of our parental task. On any given day, if we looked at the immediacy of our children's behavior and compared it with our vision for them, we could easily become discouraged. We need to remember that very seldom will any one discipline or encouragement make the difference in the lives of our children. More than anything, it is the constancy of our love, our example, our encouragement, and our discipline over the course of our children's formative years that will make the difference in their lives.

Therefore, we must stay the course. Be consistent even when it looks like the biblical principles being applied are not resulting in anything positive. We will make a difference if we persevere in doing God's will. Trust God's Word and walk out God's Word as you train up your children.

When God gave us our children, he knew that we would not be perfect parents, and yet he still gave us this task. No parent is perfect, but if we consistently follow God's Word to train up our children, great blessing will come to them. May the Lord's favor rest on your children, and on you, as you humbly pursue this great calling of parenthood!

Bibliography

Abrams, J. and S. Abrams. *Jewish Parenting: Rabbinic Insights.* Northvale, NJ: Jason Aronson, 1994.

Cohen, S. B. *Children in Halachah.* Brooklyn: Mesorah Publications, 1993.

Donin, H. H. *To Raise a Jewish Child: A Guide for Parents.* New York: Basic Books, 1977.

Ezzo, G., and A. M. Ezzo. *Let the Children Come Along the Virtuous Way.* Louisiana, MO: Growing Families International, 2002.

Fugate, J. R. *What the Bible Says About . . . Child Training.* 2nd ed. Tempe, AZ: Foundation for Biblical Research, 1996.

Kasdan, B. *God's Appointed Times: A Practical Guide for Understanding and Celebrating the Biblical Holidays.* Clarksville: Lederer Books, 1993.

Lancaster, D. T. *Restoration: Returning the Torah of God to the Disciples of Jesus.* Littleton, CO: First Fruits of Zion, 2005.

Meier, P. D. *Christian Child-Rearing and Personality Development.* Grand Rapids, MI: Baker Book House, 1977.

Switzer, T. and L. Switzer. "Parenting Is an Adventure Seminar." Unpublished manuscript.

Switzer, T. and L. Switzer. "Secrets in the Adventure of Family Life: Parenting Is an Adventure." Recording Sessions 1–7. 1997.

Ta'aseh, T. *Honoring Parents in Halachah: A Practical Guide.* Southfield, MI: Targum Press, 2004.

Telushkin, J. *The Book of Jewish Values.* New York: Bell Tower, 2000.

Twerski, A., and U. Schwartz. *Positive Parenting: Developing Your Child's Potential.* Brooklyn: Mesorah Publications, 1996.

Walsh, D. "Educating Children in the Dot-Com Age." Keynote address given at the 2001 Summer Institute for the Nova Southeastern University National Ed.D. Program for Educational Leaders.

Webster, N. *American Dictionary of the English Language.* Facsimile 1st ed. San Francisco, CA: The Foundation for American Christian Education, 1967 (1828).

PORTRAIT
OF A POWERFUL
LAST-DAY
CHRISTIAN

PORTRAIT
OF A POWERFUL
LAST-DAY
CHRISTIAN

PROPHETIC INSIGHTS FOR
SUCCESSFUL END-TIME LIVING

DAVID GARCIA

AMBASSADOR INTERNATIONAL
GREENVILLE, SOUTH CAROLINA & BELFAST, NORTHERN IRELAND

www.ambassador-international.com

Portrait of a Powerful Last-Day Christian

Prophetic Insights for Successful End-Time Living

ISBN: 978-1-62020-278-4
eISBN: 978-1-62020-381-1

Cover Design and Page Layout: Hannah Nichols
Ebook Conversion: Anna Riebe

AMBASSADOR INTERNATIONAL
Emerald House
427 Wade Hampton Blvd.
Greenville, SC 29609, USA
www.ambassador-international.com

AMBASSADOR BOOKS
The Mount
2 Woodstock Link
Belfast, BT6 8DD, Northern Ireland, UK
www.ambassador-international.com

The colophon is a trademark of Ambassador